Walk This Way

The Spirit-Led Life

By author
Byron Parson

Walk This Way:
The Spirit-Led Life

TABLE OF CONTENTS

Introduction 5

Chapter One The Plans I Have For You 15

Section One Strengthening Our Desire 23

Chapter Two A Word On The Holy Spirit 25

Chapter Three More Than We Could Ask
Or Imagine 33

Chapter Four An Age-Old Obstacle 39

Section Two Clarifying Our Views Of God 45

Chapter Five Fix Your Eyes On Jesus 47

**Section Three How Different Bible Characters
Viewed God** 57

Chapter Six Despising - Judas 59

Chapter Seven Vindictive – James And John The
Sons Of Thunder 63

Chapter Eight Condemning - Paul 69

Chapter Nine Disdainful - Gideon 73

Chapter Ten Punitive – Adam And Eve 77

Chapter Eleven Denying – Older Brother Of The Prodigal Son ... 81

Chapter Twelve Vengeful - Ahab ... 83

Chapter Thirteen Indifferent Saul ... 85

Chapter Fourteen Permitting – Jonathan And His Armor Bearer ... 89

Chapter Fifteen Enabling - Nehemiah ... 93

Chapter Sixteen – Inspiring - Caleb ... 99

Chapter Seventeen – Merciful - Elisha ... 109

Chapter Eighteen Wise - Joseph ... 115

Chapter Nineteen Loving - John ... 121

Chapter Twenty – One - Jesus ... 127

Chapter Twenty-One A Matter Of Perspective ... 133

Chapter Twenty-Two I Can See Clearly Now ... 141

Chapter Twenty-Three Setting Truth And Beauty Firmly Before You ... 159

Section Four: Overcoming The Obstacles To Following The Spirit ... 181

Chapter Twenty-Four The Practice Of Hearing And Heeding ... 183

Conclusion ... 187

INTRODUCTION

"In the past God spoke to our ancestors through the prophets at many times and in various ways, but in these last days he has spoken to us by his Son..."

Hebrews 1:1-2

"So it is written: 'The first man Adam became a living being'; the last Adam, a life-giving spirit."

1 Corinthians 15:45

"Whether you turn to the right or the left, your ears will hear a voice behind you, saying, 'This is the way; walk in it.'"

Isaiah 30:21

A fellow was stuck on his rooftop in a flood. He was praying to God for help.

Soon a man in a rowboat came by and the fellow shouted to the man on the roof, "Jump in, I can save you."

The stranded fellow shouted back, "No, it's OK, I'm praying to God, and he is going to save me."

So the rowboat went on.

Then a motorboat came by. The fellow in the motorboat shouted, "Jump in, I can save you."

To this, the stranded man said, "No thanks, I'm praying to God, and he is going to save me. I have faith."

So the motorboat went on.

Then a helicopter came by, and the pilot shouted down, "Grab this rope and I will lift you to safety."

To this, the stranded man again replied, "No thanks, I'm praying to God, and he is going to save me. I have faith."

So the helicopter reluctantly flew away.

Soon the water rose above the rooftop, and the man drowned. He went to Heaven. He finally got his chance to discuss this whole situation with God, at which point he exclaimed, "I had faith in you, but you didn't save me. You let me drown. I don't understand why!"

To this God replied, "I sent you a rowboat, a motorboat, and a helicopter. What more did you expect?"

I have loved this old story since I first heard it many years ago. It has been retold throughout the years for many reasons. I retell it here because it makes a crucial point about the importance of discerning when God is trying to communicate to us and when he is trying to lead us. The topic is certainly worthy of further examination.

There are many outstanding books on how to have a quiet time or morning devotion with God. There are Christian classics on living a disciplined life. I highly recommend them. Further still, there are volumes written on Christian character, "what would Jesus do?" and "the imitation of Christ." They are all helpful reads. This book sets out to address a different subject. That subject is: how do we develop a Spirit-led walk with God?

Some people will read this book because they are my family or friends. Thanks, Mom! Others will read it because they know me from church. There is a group of people who will pick this book up because they read every spiritual book they can get their hands on. Some just liked the cover or the title.

My hope is to touch and inspire people in various seasons of their journeys with God.

God has always desired an intimate and active relationship with us. He enjoyed an intimacy with Adam and Eve. The Bible says he strolled in the Garden of Eden with Adam and Eve, in the cool of the day. When Elisha ran for his life to the mountains of Judah, God appeared to him and whispered words of comfort and direction. The apostle

Paul reassured the Christians in Philippi, reminding them, "For it is God who works in you to will and to act in order to fulfill his good purpose." God expressed his ever presence and aid to Isaiah with these words: "Whether you turn to the right or the left, your ears will hear a voice behind you, saying, 'This is the way; walk in it.'" Throughout the scriptures, God has been present, vocal, and active in the lives of his people.

Jesus communicated the nearness of God in even more intimate ways. He said that the Father would make his home in our hearts. It's one thing to have God show up for the holidays or in times of trouble; it's a whole other matter for him to take up permanent residence. Nothing says, "I want more out of this relationship," like moving in. Is that God's toothbrush on my sink?

You never really know someone like you do when they move in. And that's the point with God. A Spirit-led relationship leads to a greater experience and recognition of Him. Knowledge of the scriptures gives us an indication of what God is like, his ways, and the pursuits of his heart. The tricky thing is that a detailed knowledge of the scriptures alone does not produce intimacy. Relational intimacy is not a matter of knowing demographic information about someone. It is a dynamic mutual responsiveness to each other.

A great example of this is Israel's King David. The Bible says David was "a man after God's own heart." Though the biblical record spends time addressing David's embrace of Scripture and commitment to spiritual disciplines, there is something else that sets him apart. It's this "after God's own heart" business. David didn't just read the scriptures; he went about his day in a moment by moment communication with the God to whom the Scriptures pointed. The Bible reveals that God communicated to David in ways David perceived, understood, and to which he responded. And at the same time, David's prayerful requests, concerns, and expressions of praise were heard by God and responded to in a way that David could discern. David had an ongoing communication and mutually responsive relationship with God.

Similarly, it was said of Enoch that "he walked with God and was no more because God had taken him away." There is no comment in Scripture about evening devotions, principles adhered to, or sacrifices made. The text only says that Enoch walked with God.

What did Enoch do? There was no Bible for him to read because the Scriptures had not yet been written. There were no prescribed sacrifices to offer, seeing that Enoch lived many years before Moses and the law. There was no temple service to attend. Enoch died over 2,200 years before Solomon's Temple was constructed. Somehow Enoch walked with God and pleased him in a manner that many others with the Bible, the Law, and the Temple could never match.

Lastly, in a prayer offered up before the raising of Lazarus from the dead, Jesus says of the father, "I know that you always hear me. I've said this for the benefit of the people that they may believe and know that you sent me." In Jesus' relationship with the Father, he knew God was actively listening as much as he was gently speaking.

It is the Holy Spirit who makes a mutually responsive relationship with God possible. It was through the Spirit that God created us in the first place. Humans, unlike any other living creature, were created with the unique capacity to commune with God. It is the Spirit who fans that communion into flames, deepens it, and strengthens it.

A Spirit-led life cannot be achieved by our works, efforts, or even sacrifices. Never has the Scripture been truer, "Not by might nor by power, but by my Spirit" (Zechariah 4:6). It is the Holy Spirit who communes with our spirit. It is the Holy Spirit who knows the mind of God. He communicates the longings of our hearts to God. He comforts us. It is through God's Spirit that in addition to our Bible knowledge, a moment by moment connection with God is made possible.

It is humbling to realize that we don't start this kind of relationship, and we are not in control of it.

"The wind blows wherever it pleases. You hear its sound, but you cannot tell where it comes from or where it is going. So it is with everyone born of the Spirit." (John 3:8)

The Spirit initiates and leads us through the superior wisdom, power, and love of God.

For me, the Spirit's leading has been anything but a straight line. He has led me to unexpected places, wonderful people, and a surprising understanding of God and life. The Spirit's leading is not likely to be any different for you, so get ready and hold on for the ride of your life!

At the start, it's God's promises that make a Spirit-led walk with Him attractive. When we don't know someone well, we're not motivated to draw close to them. But if that person is particularly attractive, famous, wealthy, or strategically connected, we might be persuaded to move in their direction. God's amazing promises are the things that pique our interest. They make us consider moving in His direction. He has what we want. He has what we need. He has what we are looking for.

Learning about God's promises is like finding a treasure map that leads to hidden gold and jewels. In the beginning, we want more of what he has to offer than we want more of Him. But as our pursuit of the treasure draws us closer to Him, our sentiment begins to change.

So much of the Spirit-led walk with God hinges on the image we hold of Him in our hearts. Seeing God accurately makes walking with Him feel safe. That's why we are told to "fix our eyes on Jesus," to "set our minds on things above", and "to set our hearts on things above." The intent of these admonitions is for us to focus our attention on the uplifting and reassuring face of Jesus. When we see God as safe and approachable, we pursue with confidence the treasures He offers.

Many treasures are surrounded by dangers and can only be pursued at our peril. In real life, treasures are kept secure by armed guards and sophisticated detection systems. In literature, treasures are guarded by mythological beasts. Though we may have heard from others that God is safe and approachable, we don't always see it that way. Based on what some of us have heard in addition to our personal experiences, dealing with God doesn't feel safe at all. The view many have of God makes them uncomfortable at the thought of getting any closer than they have to.

We see God in less than desirable ways because a tangle of emotion-laden memories and unconscious commitments distorts our view. It's our perspective that obscures our ability to see God clearly.

When we look closely at the things that distort our views of God, we will find them based on trumped-up charges, tampered evidence, and faulty logic.

We need a retrial. There needs to be a serious re-examining of the evidence. Have you ever watched a sporting event and been convinced that the player on other team was clearly out-of-bounds? Ah, the emotion, the yelling, the pointing at the television. That is, until they show the replay in super slow motion. And much to our surprise, from every camera angle, the player was clearly in bounds. The argument is over. The emotion fueled by the thoughts of biased or incompetent officials dissolves. Of course, we usually move on to complain about other aspects of the play, but nevertheless, when we take a super slow motion re-examination of how our distorted views of God came about, our perspectives change instantly.

When we see how inaccurate our view has been, we lose faith in that view, move beyond it, and are free to see the safe and approachable God, who longs to lead us to amazing heights.

For much of my life, I was enamored with the heroes of the late 1940s, '50s, and '60s, like John F. Kennedy, Robert Kennedy, Martin Luther King, and Gandhi to name a few. They all espoused the highest ideals for humanity. Unfortunately, they all died at the hands of assassins. I drew many erroneous conclusions about life, leadership, and making a difference in the world from the struggles, opposition, and ultimate fate those men shared. Little did I realize I was developing a kind of "martyrs' perspective" never intended by God. It took even more years for me to understand the implications of this point of view. It was because of this lens through which I saw everything that I would encounter many unnecessary obstacles to a truly Spirit-led life. It wasn't until I took a super slow motion re-examination of some of the conclusions I had drawn that I realized how the meaning I attached to these events distorted my view of God.

It's only when we see God as he truly is that we recognize his promptings and welcome the small voice that leads the way.

Seeing God more accurately has had a profound influence

on me. I committed myself to God many years ago, but I have grown more spiritual in the last three years than I had in the previous thirty. Now, however, I find myself drawn to Him in new ways. I am stunned by His enthusiasm, generosity, grace, and cheerfulness. I no longer have hidden reasons why God could not or would not bless me as He has those in the scriptures. The story of my life is no longer the heroic tale of surviving wave after wave of tragic events; it is a treasure hunt. It is a life of wonder and awe.

Here's what you can expect to gain along the way if you can muster the courage to look inside your heart and stay open to the powerful truths of God:

- Understanding and awareness of the great influence your view of God has on your life

- Practical tools for identifying and overcoming false beliefs

- Straightforward process for accepting empowering truths

- Skills and emotional space to bring forth untapped abilities

- Access to the Spirit's wisdom for guidance and inspiration in all aspects of your life

- Healing, wholeness, and transformation through intimacy with God

Chapter One
The Plans I Have For You

"Now to him who is able to do immeasurably more than all we ask or imagine, according to his power that is at work within us."

Ephesians 3:20

"'For I know the plans I have for you,' declares the Lord, 'plans to prosper you and not to harm you, plans to give you hope and a future.'"

Jeremiah 29:11

"He who loves with purity considers not the gift of the lover, but the love of the giver."

Thomas A. Kempis

Who will benefit from reading this book and what results should they expect from applying its strategies?

To those new to the faith, I say, what an opportunity to start off on the right path. Over the course of your life, you have a chance to move the body of believers forward in unprecedented ways. To the larger group in the mid-season of their faith, hope is on its way. This is a special group of unsung heroes. Though I have not yet had the pleasure of meeting most of them, I feel a special connection to them. They are always on my heart. You pass them on the way to work every day. They nod hello as you pass them in the train station. They are good-hearted souls. Far too many, however, are living lives of quiet desperation.

They are the disquieted majority. Some read their Bibles. Others don't. Many pray, attend church regularly and try their best to do what is right. In the quiet moments, if pressed to be perfectly honest, many would admit they are disappointed, confused, and uninspired in their experience with God.

They are committed to church, but that commitment gets harder to maintain with every year that passes. They know their Bibles well, but can't relate to the people in scripture through whom God worked so powerfully. They are willing to serve and to dutifully take on any task assigned. In their hearts, though, there are no compelling visions that have captured their imaginations and fuel their actions. They don't wake up each morning with enthusiasm and excitement at what the day may hold.

These spiritual soldiers are not going anywhere. Yet, they are barely holding on. In frustration, many have concluded that the promises they read about in scriptures are either hyperbole or reserved for the spiritually elite.

And finally, there's a small influential group I would also like to reach. This is a high energy and passionate band of people. They work hard and stay up late in service to others, but they have reached a ceiling in their effectiveness. Something in their gut tells them more of the same is not the answer. Maybe it's time to "plow up their unplowed ground" and be open to a different way of seeing things.

Many of these people have so much church and related events in their lives that it's just beginning to dawn on them that what's missing cannot be found in another activity. Others see super-religious people from a distance and are completely turned off by their lack of relatability and judgmental attitudes toward others.

Individuals in all of these groups feel a need for something. Few would describe that feeling as a longing for a Spirit-led life. Surprise! However, the moment they taste the fruit of pursuing a mutually responsive relationship with God, they will recognize it is what they were missing all along.

Fortunately, God has provided a way forward. We are going to spend the bulk of our time together learning three strategies that will help us embark on and continue in a Spirit-led life.

The first strategy strengthens our motivation for changing how we relate to God.

The second strategy identifies our prevailing view of God and corrects any misimpressions of Him.

Lastly, the third strategy delivers practical aid in overcoming obstacles to following the Spirit's lead once we've discerned His prompting.

What are the results? The first thing you will notice is a tremendous feeling of relief. That nagging sense of frustration will be gone. That cloud of confusion regarding what's going on with your life will be lifted. Taking its place will be a sense of clarity. A clear path forward will be opened up to you. The second benefit you'll reap is hope for a brighter future. With God clearly working for your benefit and nothing in your heart to hinder his efforts, the future looks better than ever.

Lastly, you'll enjoy the benefit of Spirit-enabled strength to tackle anything. God's power and presence in your life will inspire the confidence to dream big dreams (again).

Putting these strategies into practice has changed the trajectory of my life in many ways. The first change I noticed involved my prayers.

Have you ever decided to pray because you were tense and stressed about work or school, but when you left the prayer you still felt tense and stressed about work or school, and now also worried about your evangelism, an unresolved relationship, a church obligation and where you stand with God? That ain't right. Who wants to pray if that's the result?

I can relate. Years back I had an incident at work that told me something needed to change.

One of my early career positions was as a management trainee at a Fortune 500 bank. At that time, the company had a reputation for hiring to meet a certain quota and then making sure those members of "certain demographics" didn't make it through the training program. When I heard about this, I decided that was exactly the kind of rigorous challenge I needed in order to prepare myself for success in life. Every day as I walked between the massive Corinthian pillars, through the revolving door, and across the marble floor of this impressive bank, I knew I was in over my head. The volume of material to be learned, the load of work to be done, and the pervasive culture of superiority drove me to God every day, throughout the day.

I'll never forget one particularly challenging day. I had to pick up a few things at the office supply store next door to the bank. I walked the aisles of the store, not even aware of my demeanor or the expression on my face. Out of the blue, a woman in the store felt compelled to come up to me, put her hand on my shoulder, and assure me that everything was going to be all right. I thought to myself, now this is great. How am I going to let my light shine and be a source of encouragement to others when the people I'm trying to influence feel compelled to come and encourage me?

Now, I had a time of Bible study and prayer that morning. I had prayed about the difficult people and the overwhelming workload. I asked God to help me make a difference at work and in the world. I got off my knees, left the apartment, and caught the bus for downtown. On the ride, I thought some more about what awaited me at the office. I got to the building on time and climbed the steps to the main entrance. I took the elevator to the second floor, envying the tranquility of the elevator attendant. It was a short distance from the elevator to my desk. Slowly I walked this "green mile" and began my day.

What I didn't understand, however, was that I had underlying dispositions and views of myself that were negatively influencing how I prayed and the effectiveness of those prayers. I thought my prayers were to help me endure the burdens and pressures I felt. Little did I realize that God's plan for me was to transcend that whole way of being, not endure it.

My prayer life has been transformed with the Spirit's help. He has led me to a truer view of God and reminds me throughout the day to rest in His goodness. No angst, no concern, no catastrophizing, no making up unpleasant scenarios regarding the future, just a light, praise-centered, ongoing communication with God.

Previously, I strove for intensity in my prayers. This was my way of demonstrating to God the earnestness of my request. It was as if I needed to convince God to do something good. My prayers didn't have to be all night (though some were), but they had to be long enough not to appear flippant. There was a certain heaviness about my prayers that made offering them a little taxing. The most ardent prayers were brought on by some difficulty or challenge. They were couched in words of distress and deficiency. In hard times, my prayers, though heavy, provided a momentary escape from the circumstances.

Once when I was alone and still, I was prompted t ____ myself two questions. The first was whether a wise and loving God would have to be talked into doing something merciful and kind. The second question was from what kind of faith were my prayers being offered if I was worried and distressed at all, let alone while conscious of God in the very act of prayer?

Addressing those questions with an accurate view of God and the perspective of a cherished child of His has made all the difference. Now my prayers are full of acknowledgments of God's unsolicited kindness and generosity. I make simple one-time requests for his intervention, and spend any other time on the matter expressing thanks to God for answering my prayer and seeking the spiritual eyes to recognize the blessing when He has placed it in front of me. The transformation I just described happened fairly quickly. Figuring out how to make the change and uproot inaccurate beliefs without playing mind games, going into denial, or pretending not to feel what I really felt took years to discover.

How about you? Could your prayer life stand a bit of remodeling? Could you benefit from a lighter, more refreshing outlook? The Spirit stands prepared to lift and unburden, to remove obstacles and light the way.

SECTION ONE
STRENGTHENING OUR DESIRE

Chapter Two
A Word on the Holy Spirit

"If you then, though you are evil, know how to give good gifts to your children, how much more will your Father in heaven give the Holy Spirit to those who ask him?"

Luke 11:13

"My religion consists of a humble admiration of the illimitable superior spirit who reveals himself in the slight details we are able to perceive with our frail and feeble mind."

Albert Einstein

What do we mean by Holy Spirit?

Whole volumes could be filled on the topic of the Holy Spirit alone. For the purposes of this book, we will focus on the attributes and activities of the Spirit that involve our relationship with God.

One of my favorite descriptions of the Spirit comes out of the Gospel of John.

"But the Comforter, [which is] the Holy Ghost, whom the Father will send in my name, he shall teach you all things, and bring all things to your remembrance, whatsoever I have said unto you."

John 14:26

Here the Spirit is described as a person. He is a thinking being, not a force or a tool.

Jesus declares that a primary role of the Spirit is to comfort us. This is in stark contrast to descriptions of the devil as the accuser of the brothers. Are you glad that being led by the Spirit is intended to be comforting? The role of the Spirit in our lives is not to bark orders and elicit fear to get us to comply with the will of God. The Spirit brings comfort because he knows we are harassed. The implications are significant. If we desire to help others draw near God, whether a child, a friend or a stranger, there should be more comforting and less fault-finding.

I love this next verse out of the book of Romans. The Holy Spirit even helps us in our efforts to be spiritual and rely on God. Rather than stand in judgment of the length, wording or level of emotion in our prayers, the Holy Spirit fills in the gaps and expresses things we only feel and can't put into words.

"In the same way, the Spirit helps us in our weakness. We do not know what we ought to pray for, but the Spirit himself intercedes for us through wordless groans..."

Romans 8:26

The Spirit is not a hidden entity that must be conjured up. He does not reside in a heaven, which is light-years from where we sit right now. No, in every single moment of your life the Holy Spirit and the wisdom, power, and love He possesses are inside of you if you are a disciple of Jesus. He does not leave when you fail and return when you do a good deed. The Holy Spirit is not a process that is activated and deactivated based on our behavior or performance. The Holy Spirit is a person, devoted to our well-being and more loyal to us than we are to ourselves.

"What? know ye not that your body is the temple of the Holy Ghost [which is] in you, which ye have of God, and ye are not your own?"

1 Corinthians 6:19

"Now the Lord is the Spirit: and where the Spirit of the Lord is, there is freedom."

2 Corinthians 3:17

A Spirit-led life is a life of freedom. His aim is to free us from rules and regulations, both our own and those imposed externally, and inspire thoughts and actions motivated by compassion and the joy of seeing others prosper.

The Holy Spirit frees us from envy, jealousy, resentment, and the desire to progress at someone else's expense. He does this by reminding us that we are already rich in Christ, loved and valued beyond measure.

"But the Advocate, the Holy Spirit, whom the Father will send in my name, will teach you all things and will remind you of everything I have said to you."

John 14:26

Paul tells us in Romans chapter 15 that the Holy Spirit brings power into our lives. This is a strength or capacity to hold on to the peace and joy that God provides.

"Now the God of hope fill you with all joy and peace in believing, that ye may abound in hope, through the power of the Holy Ghost."

Romans 15:3

"And the spirit of the LORD shall rest upon him, the spirit of wisdom and understanding, the spirit of counsel and might, the spirit of knowledge and of the fear of the LORD;"

Isaiah 11:2

In short, the Spirit leads, comforts, speaks, preaches, convicts, inspires, reminds, teaches, moves hearts and makes up for what the law could not accomplish with weakened human flesh. Remember this distinction; the role of the Holy Spirit is to convict the world and to comfort God's children.

How does He communicate?

- Through bringing understanding of the scriptures- John 14:26 Ephesians 6:17

- Through the mouth of prophets- 1 Peter 1:21

- Changing natural phenomenon- Psalm 104:30

- Speaking intelligible languages- Act 2:4

- Groans- Romans 8:26

- Impressions- John 6:44

- Stirring up a person's spirit – Haggai 1:14

- Visions- Acts 2:17

- Dreams- Acts 2:17

What kind of responses can we have to the Spirit?

Most often the Spirit's intent for communicating with us is to have us follow His direction. For the rare person who actually senses the Spirit's direction, they will have to choose between obedience and disobedience. The most common challenge for most of us is to orient our lives in such a way to hear him at all. But on those occasions where it's clear that He's beginning to communicate with us, we would do well to wait, listen, acknowledge and obey. Choice also brings the option to resist, quench, disobey and outright blaspheme. As a matter of fact, the only thing the Bible says we can do that is not forgivable is to blaspheme the Holy Spirit. Note to self: Don't do that!

Exactly how does one commit this unforgivable sin? We know that God has forgiven murderers, rapists, prostitutes, thieves, assassins, etc. Therefore, most scholars believe blasphemy of the Holy Spirit to be resisting the prompting of the Spirit to turn to God for one's entire life. Because after we pass from this world, there is no opportunity to repent.

The boy prophet Samuel is a good example for us in orienting ourselves to respond faithfully to the Spirit's lead. It became clear to the old prophet Eli that God was attempting to communicate to the young Samuel. Eli gave Samuel directions that he faithfully followed. Samuel went to his room and lay on the bed. There he waited. When he sensed that God was speaking, he acknowledges Him saying, "Speak Lord, for your servant is listening." Despite being charged with an unpleasant task, he faithfully obeyed and spoke the words of chastisement to Eli that God had commanded him.

Unfortunately, the crowd to which Steven spoke was an example of how not to respond to God. Here is Stephen's rebuke of their obstinacy:

"You stiff-necked people! Your hearts and ears are still uncircumcised. You are just like your ancestors: You always resist the Holy Spirit! "

Acts 7:51

The crowd continued in their resistance and active disobedience. Their hostility toward the Spirit ended with them stoning Steven to death.

As powerful as the Holy Spirit is, He does not take us over and make us do things against our will. He prompts. He reveals. He disturbs. He delights. But at the end of the day, the choice to obey is always our own.

CHAPTER THREE
MORE THAN WE COULD ASK OR IMAGINE

The promises that await us when we walk with God are rich and numerous. It's amazing that we have contented ourselves for so long with so much less. Yes, adhering to principles is much better than a lawless existence. And committing to a purpose greater than ourselves is its own reward. But the promises unleashed in a Spirit-led life are without equal.

"What no eye has seen, what no ear has heard, and what no human mind has conceived — the things God has prepared for those who love him"

2 Corinthians 2:9.

Can we love God and not follow where he leads?

We are told that God draws us to himself with "cords of loving kindness."

Here are a few of my favorite promises God uses to draw us closer to him:

"I am your shield, your very great reward."

Genesis 15:1

When the Israelites left Egyptian captivity, Pharaoh's army was in hot pursuit. Defenseless and untrained in the art of war, the Israelites needed protection. God provided that protection in the form of a pillar of cloud by day and a pillar of fire by night. Both pillars moved at irregular intervals. Sometimes they stayed in place for a night. At other times, they remained in place for weeks. The point is, in order to stay protected, the Israelites had to move and follow the lead of the pillars. When the Spirit leads, we stay protected as we follow.

Consider the example of the sons of Jacob. God had promised that the children of those who have faith in Him would never go hungry. And yet in Genesis, we find Jacob and his sons threatened with starvation as their homeland suffered a severe drought. God was still Jacob's shield and protection. He had provided for an abundance of food, but Jacob and his sons had to move from their homeland to Egypt to enjoy God's provisions. What if Jacob had insisted that God provided where he was, in his homeland? What if he refused to believe that everyone else might starve, but not him because he trusted in God? Jacob's faith included following God's lead and not stubbornly requiring God to bless on Jacob's terms. This reminds me of one of my favorite Will Rogers quotes, "Even if you're on the right track, you'll get run over if you just sit there." Being Spirit-led requires us to be flexible and open to the world beyond our little hamlets.

"I can do all things through God, who gives me strength."

Philippians 4:13

"Whoever believes in me, as Scripture has said, rivers of living water will flow from within them."

John 7:38

"I pray that the eyes of your heart may be enlightened in order that you may know the hope to which he has called you, the riches of his glorious inheritance in the saints, and his incomparably great power for us who believe. That power's like the working of his mighty strength, which he exerted in Christ when he raised him from the dead and seated him at the right hand in the heavenly realms, far above all rulers and authority, power and dominion and every title that can be given, not only in the present age but also in the one to come."

Ephesians 1:18-22

"I pray that out of his glorious riches he may strengthen you with power through his Spirit in your inner being so that Christ may dwell in your hearts through faith. And I pray that you, being rooted and established in love, may have power, together with all the saints, to grasp how wide and long and high and deep is the love of Christ, and to know this love that surpasses knowledge, that you may be filled to the measure of all the fullness of God."

"Now to him who is able to do immeasurably more than all we ask or imagine, according to his power that is at work within us, to him be (the) glory in the church and in Christ Jesus throughout all generations, forever and ever! Amen."

Ephesians 3:16-21

"... until we all reach unity in the faith and in the knowledge of the Son of God and become mature, attaining to the whole measure of the fullness of Christ. Then we will no longer be infants, tossed back and forth by the waves, and blown here and there by every wind of teaching and the cunning and craftiness of men in their deceitful scheming. Instead, speaking the truth in love, we will in all things grow up into him who is the Head, that is, Christ."

Ephesians 4:13

"For in Christ all the fullness of the Deity lives in bodily form, and you have been given fullness in Christ, who was the head over every power and authority."

Colossians 2:12

I know that's a lot of scriptures. But ask yourself, "Am I experiencing these promises in my life today?" You'll notice that these promises are largely tied to our active believing, obedient love, and relational response to God.

We will explore in some detail later the richness and, if you will, the mind-blowing implications of the promise of "obtaining the whole measure of the fullness of Christ." And what it means to be "filled to the measure of all the fullness of God." Oh yeah, and on the way to the richest blessings of all, "the fullness of God," Jesus promises tangible rewards. He says,

"No one who is left home or brothers or sisters or mother or father or children or fields for me and the Gospel will fail to receive a hundred times as much in this present age: homes, brothers, sisters, mothers, children and fields -- and with them persecutions, and in the age to come eternal life."

Mark 10:29

The promise of homes and fields are to keep us engaged and motivated, believing in his goodness, so that we will, in the end, pursue the greatest blessing of all, "the fullness of God." Don't get me wrong, when you're broke and all alone, homes, fields, brothers, and sisters look pretty good and are nothing to sneeze at. We see a similar kind of joy in our children at Christmastime. We give them the latest video game or gadget as presents while we are trying to raise tens of thousands of dollars for their college education. The video game may be despised as antiquated by the next Christmas while a college education will serve them all their lives. Similarly, the miraculous home we thought we'd never own may be despised later as burdensome and limiting as we hunger for the greater things of the heart, spirit, and soul. But something has spoiled our appetite for these very blessings.

Chapter Four
An Age-Old Obstacle

"...but we preach Christ crucified: a stumbling block to Jews and foolishness to Gentiles."

1 Corinthians 1:23

"You study the Scriptures diligently because you think that in them you have eternal life. These are the very Scriptures that testify about me, yet you refuse to come to me to have life."

John 5:39-40

As an old saying goes, "Good is the enemy of great." How true this is of our spiritual journey. It's usually not murder or embezzlement that retards our spiritual progress. We often succumb to the same things our forefathers did throughout the ages. In the past, people could not embrace the teachings of the prophets because of their commitment to the traditions of their ancestors. The Israelites had a hard time accepting the teachings of John the Baptist and Jesus because of their commitment to the Law. For generations, the most upright among the Jewish people considered obedience to the Law as paramount. It was their father's tradition of following the Law that brought the people out of a brutal and barbaric past. Consequently, they had no intention of letting go of their traditions. But by adhering to the traditions, they forfeited any opportunity for something better. People failed to hear Jesus at a heart level because of their commitment to the law and prophets. The people weren't just stubborn. Earlier generations suffered horribly for neglecting the words of the Law and the prophets. After receiving such stiff and painful discipline from the Lord, they had no intention of ever letting go of the words of the laws or the prophets. And yet in refusing to let go, they could not embrace the very Son of God to which the law and the prophets pointed.

We face a similar challenge in our spiritual walk. For most of us, turning to God involved a commitment to a form of morality far superior to the standards of which we had been living. We definitely changed. Some of us bear in our hearts and minds and sometimes on our bodies the scars of our previous ways. We once lived unprincipled and undisciplined lives. But we repented of our worldliness so we could live the way God would have us live. We accepted the high principles of honesty, modesty, purity, etc. that were preached to us. All in all, these new ways were obviously superior to the often self-serving behaviors that ruled our lives. Nevertheless, they all fall short in one important way. If God calls us to something beyond the present rules, we are likely not to understand (His ways are higher than our ways, and His thoughts are higher than our thoughts), and chalk up the impression to a random thought. This is how Peter wrestled the Spirit's c?

Peter walked with Jesus. But, when in a vision he was called to kill an unclean animal and eat it, his reply was, "Surely not, Lord. I have never eaten anything unclean." Can you see the problem he was facing? Peter says, "Surely, not I, Lord." He believes he is speaking to the Lord, and yet he believes his moral, biblical, and principled commitment to not defiling himself is to take precedence over the still small voice that said, "This is the way. Eat it." Peter showed moral integrity when he rejected eating the unclean food. He was hungry. His meal was still cooking. He showed great restraint.

It was even biblical for Peter to refuse to eat unclean food. He could have quoted dozens of scriptures to support his conviction. It just wasn't the will of God for Peter to reject the "unclean" food at that moment. We all know the character, discipline, and self-control required to fast, but for Peter, refusing to eat at this time was not the will of God. Do you see the quandary in which Peter found himself?

Have you ever been in this situation before? You're driving and you approach an intersection with a traffic officer. You clearly see the light is red as you approach the intersection. You know all the rules of the road regarding red lights, but as your car gets to the intersection, the police officer waves you forward. The light says stop, but the man says go. In situations like these, we have to remember consciously that the authority of the officer on the scene outweighs the rule of the road to stop at all red lights.

Not only will we have to get past the obstacles of our cultural and religious habits, but we also have to overcome ourselves. The following highlight challenges for which we will need good friends and a supportive community to move beyond:

- Ascribing to the Spirit one's own personal ambitions and desires

- Being told something you don't understand

- Being told something you don't want to do

- Being told to do something you don't think is appropriate

- Being told to do something inconvenient

- Being told to do something dangerous

- Being told to do something that will result in conflict

- Being told to do something that may result in a personal loss

You'll recognize a common theme with the Spirit's leadership of your life. In general, you'll be called to love more people, more often, more deeply, and more selflessly than you ever have before. The Spirit calls us to be our most authentic selves. This "true you" may be different from what people have come to expect from you or believe about you.

I feel this call in my workplace. It is a place of business, not a social organization. Loving my demanding and difficult co-workers especially with deadlines looming often feels counterproductive. Love and consideration can give the appearance of being soft. This is not a trait for which most take-charge, make-it-happen leaders are known.

If you don't feel a similar pull in your spiritual life now, you likely will at some point in the future. Whether it is work, school, family, or community, the Spirit will call us all well beyond our comfort zone.

But when you fully embrace the truth, that the only way to walk with God is being led by the Spirit moment by moment, listening for God's voice, and heeding it, a great burden will be lifted. The challenge will become an adventure. Hesitation and fear will be overtaken by clarity and understanding.

SECTION TWO
CLARIFYING OUR VIEWS OF GOD

CHAPTER FIVE
FIX YOUR EYES ON JESUS

"Fix your eyes on Jesus, the pioneer, and perfector of the faith."

Hebrews 12:2

"Set your hearts on things above, where Christ is, seated at the right hand of God. Set your minds on things above, not on earthly things."

Colossians 3:1-2

We are encouraged to fix our eyes on Jesus, but how we see Jesus differs from person to person. How we see God varies from person to person. The very act of concentrating on God is designed to awaken, empower, and inspire us. However, that is not the case for far too many people. Their thoughts of God evoke nothing positive and sometimes bring shame, repulsion or worse.

In more areas of my life than I wanted to admit, I also had views of God that were not altogether accurate. I knew the Bible expressed these amazing realities about God, His ways, and His promises. But I had to ask myself, "Why am I not walking on cloud nine all the time?" "Why do little things bother me?" "How can I worry about anything in the light of God's promises to protect and bless me?" "Why am I not brimming over with enthusiasm every moment?"

Something was keeping the knowledge of these promises and truths from having the logical uplifting effect on me. They say admitting you have a problem is half the solution. When I asked myself how I felt about God, it was always, "Great!" But I knew something was off.

I found the best way for me to really see what I believed about God at any given moment was to ask myself, "How do you think God feels about you right now?"

I found that my answer showed the purer, less filtered, indication of my faith regarding God at that moment.

One day I was reading a book on leadership and influence when I turned the page and came across a table that hit me like a ton of bricks.

It was a table that listed different levels of consciousness. From my perspective, the chart was showing different ways of viewing God, and it nailed me right where I sat. The views and the insights the table brought forth explained so much about what I was experiencing and not experiencing. I had seen for a long time that the scriptures described God as love. I saw many of the Bible characters moved by God's love. After examining the table, I realized that not only did my thoughts about how God felt toward me expose my true faith, but it explained so much more about a host of dynamics playing out in my life.

The scriptures became brighter, deeper, and more vivid than ever before. In page after page, I saw God revealing a continuum of beliefs about Him through the Bible characters and the way they process the events in their lives.

I came to understand that whatever anyone holds to be true about God determines the lens through which they see everything. How we see God creates our dominant attitude toward life. It determines our emotional state and our sense of what is going to happen to us. Our view of God has a tremendous influence on how we process and respond to life's events. How we see God will affect the quality and outcome of our life, relationships, and career as well as much of our mental and physical health. wow!

Pretty much how we see God affects everything, not the least of which is how we see ourselves.

Below is a table showing how our perceptions of God create in us different life views, developmental levels, dominant emotions, and the process by which we are likely to attempt affecting our present situation.

God-View	Life-View	Habit of Being	Dominant Emotion	Process of Life
One	Complete	Joy	Serenity	Transfiguration
Loving	Benign	Love	Reverence	Revelation
Wise	Meaningful	Reason	Understanding	Abstraction
Merciful	Harmonious	Acceptance	Forgiveness	Transcendence
Inspiring	Hopeful	Willingness	Optimism	Intention
Enabling	Satisfactory	Neutrality	Trust	Release
Permitting	Feasible	Courage	Affirmation	Empowerment
Indifferent	Demanding	Pride	Scorn	Inflation
Vengeful	Antagonistic	Anger	Hate	Aggression
Denying	Disappointing	Desire	Craving	Enslavement
Punitive	Frightening	Fear	Anxiety	Withdrawal
Disdainful	Tragic	Grief	Regret	Despondency
Condemning	Hopeless	Apathy	Despair	Abdication
Vindictive	Evil	Guilt	Blame	Destruction
Despising	Miserable	Shame	Humiliation	Elimination

(Power vs Force)

You will notice in the table, moving from the bottom up, that it's not until halfway up the list that the perceptions of God and their accompanying levels of maturity and dominant emotional states become even remotely positive. Though the lower half is still negative, as you move up to the midpoint of the table, each perspective, or aspect of faith, becomes decreasingly debilitating. They become increasingly powerful, energetic, liberating and closer to the truth. Through the rest of this section of the book, we are going to look at Bible characters who serve as archetypes of the different God Views. We will see how the course and outcome of their lives were shaped by what they believed about God.

The table uses some descriptions that need defining. Let's discuss the meaning of these terms so we are all on the same page.

God view

Here, we simply mean how we see God at any given moment. It's the image of God we hold in our mind's eye. Fundamentally, our God view is what we think God is like.

Of the many different ways, we can discern our view of God, one of the most revealing is to describe how we think God sees us at a given moment. Some of us may have to chew on this for a bit. But think about it. How a person feels about us usually says more about them than it says about us. Their feelings are but the response to how we either meet or conflict with some value system, temperament, expectation, or personal history of theirs. They feel about us a certain way because of who they are. Therefore, how we think God feels about us says so much about what we believe he's really like.

Let's compare what a believer might habitually say about God with what they would respond with if asked how God feels about them at the moment. What does God think of them? The difference is sometimes highlighted in our conversations with each other. When we ask each other, "How are you doing in your relationship with God?" The answer is as much a commentary on how we view God as it is any behavior or attitudes we may or may not be exhibiting.

Can you describe your relationship with God without starting with a lament of your sins and weaknesses? Doesn't that sentiment suggest that you see God as primarily a fault finder or accuser? The Bible does describe someone like that, but it's not referring to God.

Life View

By life, we're talking about a person's general outlook on life. What life is like to them.

This can be illustrated by completing this sentence stem:

"Life is ___."

Some would say:

Life is hard.

Life is painful.

Life is a bowl of cherries.

Life is a dance.

Life is a blessing.

Life is disappointing.

Life is a sick joke.

Life is a _____, and then you die.

It would be difficult to think God views us in loving, inspiring and merciful ways and conclude that life is hard or disappointing.

What we consistently say about life is the result of how we view God and his sovereign rule and control of the universe.

<u>Habit of being</u>

Think of "habit of being" like this:

When asked, "What is _____ (insert a person's name) like?" The response is a description of what that person is generally like. In other words, it is their habit of being.

Someone else can usually give us a more objective assessment of our habit of being than we can ourselves. It's true that other people don't know what we are thinking or how we feel, but they can see how we act and carry ourselves.

Dominant Emotion

By this, we mean the feeling within you that is most prevalent throughout the day above all your other emotions.

"Most of the time I feel ____."

It's the emotion we experience most often and over the longest periods of time in an average day.

In Latin, the word for emotion is "emovere," meaning to move out.

We are always moving on a physical plane according to the dominant emotion within.

Life process

By life process, we are communicating a combination of a person's common thoughts, conclusions, decisions and actions taken in response to life's daily encounters.

Whether the situations are viewed as opportunities or demands depends on the person's God view.

Life process is our typical way of handling the things that come our way.

We can:

- Become threatened or inspired

- Become protective or inviting

- Make plans or act on impulse

- Mentally script a defense of our actions or inactivity

- Solicit help or go it alone

- Retreat or advance

- Advocate or retire

Our life process is what we usually end up doing or not doing and how we go about it.

In the next chapter, we're going to take a look at several Bible characters and their lives, decisions and thoughts, demonstrating vividly how our view of God influences our life, our habit of being, our dominant emotion, and how we process life's events.

SECTION THREE
How Different Bible Characters Viewed God

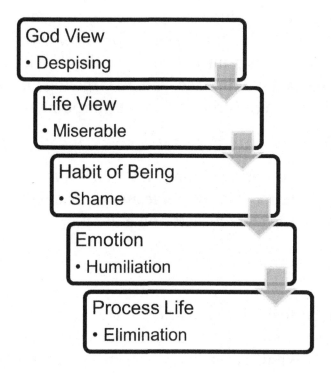

Definition: Despise — to consider something not worthwhile to hold on to or to save. We can despise a piece of paper stuck to the bottom of our shoe. We quickly discard it, considering it worthless. In Genesis, the Bible says Esau "despised his birthright." He didn't even see it as worth a bowl of stew. He despised it by not seeing the value in holding on to it.

Much has been written about how Jesus loved the twelve apostles. Even the other apostles couldn't discern a difference in Jesus' affection towards Judas. At the Lord's Supper, the apostles had no idea that Judas would betray Jesus. The fatal flaw of Judas was not how God saw him or even how Jesus treated him, but rather, how Judas saw God. Though Judas was given the keys to eternal life in the words and person of Jesus, he discarded them for thirty silver coins. Judas never valued all that Jesus preached and taught about acceptance, forgiveness, and turning the other cheek. So when Judas came to realize the depth of his sin in betraying Jesus, he didn't see God as forgiving and one who would also turn the other cheek. At this point, his life view is miserable.

"When Judas, who had betrayed him, saw that Jesus was condemned, he was seized with remorse and returned the thirty silver coins to the chief priests and elders."

Matthew 27:3

The shame Judas feels is unbearable. He is utterly humiliated. "I have sinned," he said, "for I have betrayed innocent blood." "What is that to us?" they replied. "That's your responsibility." Fearing he would be forever unacceptable to God, the only way to eliminate this pain was to eliminate himself. Judas hanged himself.

Those who see God as one who finds no value in them will often self-sabotage and find themselves in many self-destructive behaviors. Almost by definition, suicidal temptations flow from a distorted sense that one's life is not worth the time of day to God. Isn't it amazing that one of David's struggles was that God paid too much attention to him? Despite having sinned as grievously as anyone in scripture, David never gave any thought to giving up and taking his life. Was it that David had unshakeable self-esteem which pulled him through the dark times? No. In Psalm 51:5 he described himself as so sin-prone that it must have started at his very conception. Despite this, he says "What is man, that you are mindful of him, the son of man that you care for him? You made him a little lower than the angels and crowned him with glory and honor."

Psalm 8:4-5

David thought God viewed man as just short of heavenly and loved them as his own.

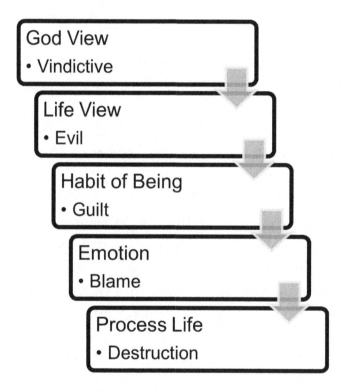

God View
- Vindictive

Life View
- Evil

Habit of Being
- Guilt

Emotion
- Blame

Process Life
- Destruction

Definition: Vindictive — showing malicious, ill will, and a desire to hurt; motivated by spite. There is no desire for justice, redemption or rehabilitation in vindictiveness. It is a mean-spirited need and desire to see someone suffer.

In Luke 9:49-56, we are given a picture of James and John badly misreading the nature of God:

> An argument started among the disciples as to which of them would be the greatest. Jesus, knowing their thoughts, took a little child and had him stand beside him. Then he said to them, 'Whoever welcomes this little child in my name welcomes me; and whoever welcomes me welcomes the one who sent me. For he who is least among you all—he is the greatest.'"

> 'Master,' said John, 'we saw a man driving out demons in your name, and we tried to stop him because he is not one of us.'

> 'Do not stop him,' Jesus said, 'for whoever is not against you is for you.'

> As the time approached for him to be taken up to heaven, Jesus resolutely set out for Jerusalem. And he sent messengers on ahead, who went into a Samaritan village to get things ready for him; but the people there did not welcome him because he was heading for Jerusalem. When the disciples James and John saw this, they asked, 'Lord, do you want us to call fire down from heaven to destroy them?' But Jesus turned and rebuked them. And he said, 'You do not know what kind of spirit you are of, for the Son of Man did not come to destroy men's lives, but to save them.' And they went to another village.

Jesus had resolutely set about to accomplish God's will, and James and John took note of this definiteness of purpose. The people of the village refused to welcome the Son of God, and James and John made note of this as well. Jesus moved on to the next village with no ill will. James and John missed that one. God was not one to be interfered with as they saw it. To do so was evil. Life was full of these little evils, ever attempting to thwart God's will. In their view, these people are to blame for standing in God's way, and He would want this obstruction removed.

At this point, James and John desire to help God's will move along. In a gesture motivated by the desire to serve God, they make an improbable recommendation: "Jesus, would you like us to destroy this and its people for their wicked obstruction of God's plans?" The reply that Jesus gives is more than no. He immediately knew that they had not rightly seen or understood the true ways of God. Jesus turns and rebukes them. James and John had not just made an error of judgment; their recommendation revealed a spirit that was the polar opposite of God's Spirit. Jesus said, "You do not know what kind of spirit you are of." I love this phrase.

Your view of God's will and what you have concluded of His nature is off-base. God is resolutely set on saving lives, not destroying them.

How do James and John end up with thoughts of God as vindictive? Up until this point in the gospel of John, there is no record of Jesus having rebuked a Pharisee or a teacher of the law. There has been no thunderous condemnation of the Roman government. Jesus had not made a comment on the crime and violence that was rampant in Jerusalem at that time. Therefore, James and John could not have picked up this vindictive trait from their observations of Jesus.

What we are left to draw from is the personal history of James and John, their understanding of the Old Testament, the God of the Old Testament, and the stories and traditions that had been passed down throughout the generations. When Jesus called the 12 disciples to him and designated the Apostles, he gave James and John the nickname Sons of Thunder. Evidently, there was something in their character and temperament that tended toward explosive reactions to circumstances and provocations. But in fairness, those of us who have some knowledge of the Old Testament can recall many times where God both threatened to destroy a nation and a people and followed-up with their destruction.

What James and John may not have understood from these accounts, along with many others, was that God was surgically removing a cancerous element from the Earth to preserve the hope of a righteous nation through whom the Messiah could come. Holy threats leveled against these nations were always motivated by a desire to get them to repent. Their destruction was purely for the preservation of humanity. And so rather than standing in awe of a loving and patient God, who would endure rebellion for generations and act only to preserve humanity, they concluded that God felt slighted and acted to avenge Himself.

Nevertheless, at this point, James and John held this vindictive view of God, and from that view, they had a pattern in their lives of responding to events with violence.

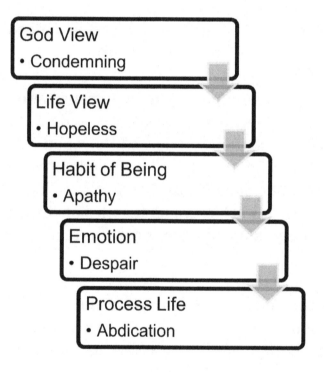

God View
• Condemning

Life View
• Hopeless

Habit of Being
• Apathy

Emotion
• Despair

Process Life
• Abdication

Definition - Condemn 1. to express an unfavorable or adverse judgment on; indicate strong disapproval of; censure, 2. to pronounce to be guilty, sentenced to punishment, 3. to judge or pronounce to be unfit for use or service, i.e. to condemn an old building 4. to declare incurable.

The Apostle Paul offers a glimpse into a dark period in his ministry life. Something happened on one of his missionary journeys in the province of Asia. He gives us a picture of his view of life, emotions, and prospects for the future in a statement recorded in 2 Corinthians 1:8-9:

"We do not want you to be uninformed, brothers and sisters, about the troubles we experienced in the province of Asia. We were under great pressure, far beyond our ability to endure, so that we despaired of life itself. Indeed, we felt we had received the sentence of death."

In that dark hour, Paul summed up their interpretation, perspective or belief about the situation by saying, "... in our hearts, we felt the sentence of death." He espoused a similar sentiment in 1 Co 4:9 where he looked across to the experience of other apostles as well and concluded, "For it seems to me that God has put us apostles on display at the end of the procession, like those condemned to die in the arena."

Let's look at how this sense of condemnation affected Paul. Notice his comment that he felt a pressure beyond his ability. That's just another way of expressing hopelessness. There was nothing he could do to better his situation. Emotionally, they were in complete despair, and so much so, that they wanted it all just to end. They were ready to give up not only on the mission but life itself.

Here Paul has given us a glimpse into his emotions and thought process before the truth of God enters the picture.

After the fact, he reasons that since God is a God who raises the dead, even a sentence of death can be met with hope, energy, encouragement and an expectation of better things to come.

In the end, Paul makes it clear that because a loving God is present, we do not have to rely on ourselves.

This is another way of saying we don't have to live as though God were not present or did not care for us and work daily for our good.

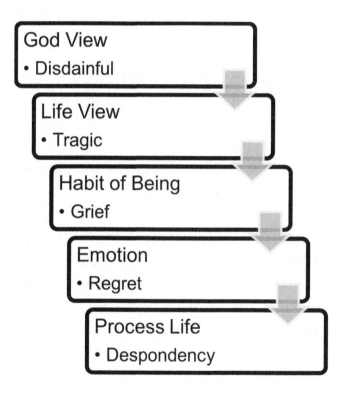

God View
• Disdainful

Life View
• Tragic

Habit of Being
• Grief

Emotion
• Regret

Process Life
• Despondency

Definition: Disdainful— "to look down upon, to consider something unworthy of notice."

"...but if the Lord is with us, why has all this happened to us? Where are all his wonders that our ancestors told us about when they said, 'Did not the Lord bring us up out of

Egypt?' But now the Lord has abandoned us and given us into the hand of Midian."

Judges 6:13

Gideon clearly is grieving the loss of God's help, favor, and esteem. He voices for many the hurts, concerns, disappointments and exasperation of feeling abandoned by God.

Why has all this happened to us? Why do we find ourselves in such a tragic situation? You abandoned us, and we are subject to terror.

It's that decaying sense that God has deemed your life and struggles unworthy of his attention or efforts.

This disdain is like passing a department store display that does not even turn your head. It completely fails to grab your attention. Despite the crushing situation that Israel finds itself in, to Gideon, God has passed them by without valuing their situation as worthy of His attention.

Gideon summed up the tragedy of Midian's brutal treatment of Israel as, "Why has all this happened to us?" The present oppression is compared to the wonders and miracles that accompanied God's presence and favor in years gone by.

All of God's miraculous interventions of the past were called to his mind, but the thought of God's present view of Israel ruled the day. God's present lack of consideration leaves Gideon despondent, completely inactive, and doing absolutely nothing that could change Israel's plight.

Israel is hiding in caves, and Gideon is hiding in a winepress. So strong are the feelings of abandonment that Gideon pours out his complaint to "the angel of the Lord," the very instrument of God's attention, communication, and intervention.

Fortunately, the story doesn't end there. Gideon comes to believe that God was present and had plans to rescue Israel from Midian. Once persuaded, his lethargy is lifted, and he swings into action.

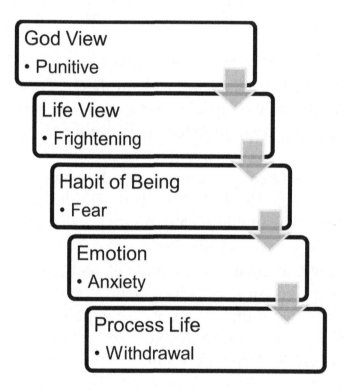

God View
• Punitive

Life View
• Frightening

Habit of Being
• Fear

Emotion
• Anxiety

Process Life
• Withdrawal

Definition: Punitive - intended to punish someone or something; extremely or unfairly severe or high.

The book of Genesis relates this as the well-known story of the first sin, which took place in the Garden of Eden.

"When the woman saw that the fruit of the tree was good for food and pleasing to the eye, and also desirable for gaining wisdom, she took some and ate it. She also gave some to her husband, who was with her, and he ate it. Then the eyes of both of them were opened, and they realized they were naked; so they sewed fig leaves together and made coverings for themselves."

Genesis 1:6-7

Before eating the forbidden fruit, Adam and Eve walked about freely in the garden, naked and with no shame. They had no shame in their relationship with each other nor did they have any shame in their fellowship with the Lord.

Though the Lord explained that there would be negative consequences for eating the forbidden fruit, He did not say that He personally would punish them.

You and I have both warned someone about handling a sharp item so as not to cut themselves. If, however, they did cut themselves, we didn't cause it to happen. As a result, they would find no reason to change their feelings about us and our relationship with them.

For Adam and Eve, this was not just a cause and effect incident. Something had now changed in the relationship between them and their creator, provider, protector. Adam and Eve assumed that they were no longer "safe" in God's sight. They needed to hide or withdraw fellowship from Him for fear of some harm at his hand.

God did pronounce the result of their disobedience. What we don't know is if this was a decision on God's part or him merely explaining how life works, like someone describing what would happen if you threw a rock in the air and stood under it. What we do know is that Adam and Eve viewed God as the source of any punishment and attempted to separate themselves from Him as a result.

CHAPTER ELEVEN
DENYING – OLDER BROTHER OF THE PRODIGAL SON

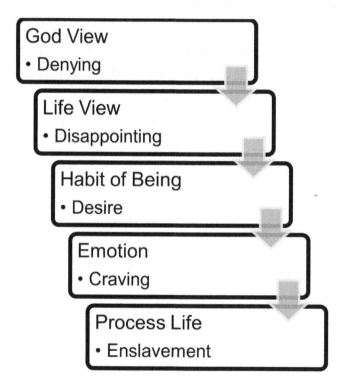

Definition: Deny - to actively prevent a situation from occurring or something from being obtained.

The older brother of the prodigal son is a good example of

one who views God as denying. He was the son of a wealthy landowner. The scripture reveals his father to be a kind and generous soul. The elder son was the sole heir of the estate, but when his long-lost brother returns, rather than rejoicing, the older brother is disappointed in the father.

Despite all of the father's generosity, the oldest son resents not being provided a young goat to celebrate with his friends. The father tells him not only could he have a young goat, but that everything he owned belonged to him.

So strong is the desire to celebrate with his friends that the fixation on a goat is not even dissolved in the light of his brother's safe return.

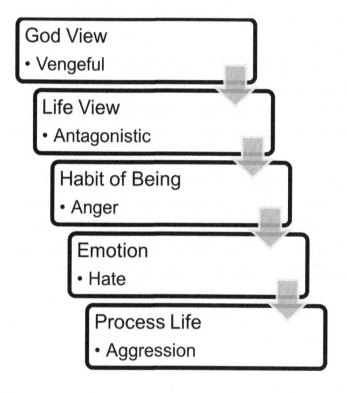

Definition: Vengeful - assumes a slight has occurred, and there are desires for equal or greater retaliation.

Second Chronicles 18 describes an altercation between the Kings of Israel and Aram.

At the beginning of this incident, the king of Israel already feels that the king of Aram has taken land that belongs to him. Though peace has settled in the land for the last three years, the king is ready for a fight. The king of Aram was minding his own business. However, the king of Israel has antagonistic views toward him and is preparing to provoke a conflict. Additionally, the king of Israel is angry with the prophet Micah. According to the king, he only prophesizes bad; he never prophesies anything good for the king.

Do you know anyone who sees life and everyone in it as an adversary, a competitor, or threat? Those who see God as vengeful often speak of God being "disrespected" and they also refuse ever to be disrespected.

In a lapse of royal behavior, King Ahab declared to Jehoshaphat that he "hates the prophet of the Lord," who is merely a messenger of God. The king's take on God and life produces an atmosphere of aggression. Ahab is ready to fight the king of Aram. He wants to draw Jehoshaphat into hostilities. Ahab hates Micah. He orders Jedediah to slap Micah in a display of aggression. Lastly, Ahab throws Micah in prison with nothing but bread and water.

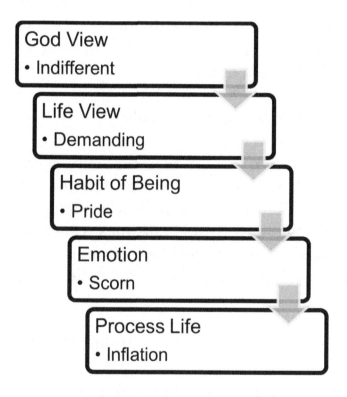

Definition: Indifferent - having no particular interest or sympathy; unconcerned.

When the Israelites saw that their situation was critical and that their army was hard pressed, they hid in caves and thickets, among the rocks, and in pits and cisterns. Some Hebrews even crossed the Jordan to the land of Gad and Gilead.

Saul remained at Gilgal, and all the troops with him were quaking with fear. He waited seven days, the time set by Samuel; but Samuel did not come to Gilgal, and Saul's men began to scatter. So he said, 'Bring me the burnt offering and the fellowship offerings.' And Saul offered up the burnt offering. Just as he finished making the offering, Samuel arrived, and Saul went out to greet him.

'What have you done?' asked Samuel.

Saul replied, 'When I saw that the men were scattering, and that you did not come at the set time, and that the Philistines were assembling at Mikmash, I thought, Now the Philistines will come down against me at Gilgal, and I have not sought the Lord's favor. So I felt compelled to offer the burnt offering.'

1 Samuel 13:6:12

The pressures that Saul feels and the actions he takes can all be traced back to his view of God surrounding this event.

The situation is critical. Time is not on Israel's side. The enemy is advancing, and God has not acted. The sacrifice needs to be offered but should only be offered by a priest.

As the representative of God, Samuel's failure to show is the same as God's failure to show, as far as Saul is concerned. Without God, the demands of the situation fall on Saul. Since God has not provided the priest, he must take matters into his own hands.

It's all up to him. But no sooner did Saul offer the sacrifice, when Samuel arrives, the priest God had intended to offer the sacrifice all along. When confronted, Saul does not say, "Oh no, what have I done?" Rather, he goes into a monologue about all the things he had done in Samuel's absence. Saul's pride is on full display in his recounting of all that he had stepped up to do. Not only does he take credit for his actions like he was saving the day, but he also begins to blame Samuel for not performing his duties and not being there when he was needed.

All these pressures Saul feels and the accusations he lays on Samuel come in large part because he viewed God as indifferent in that critical moment. We can compare Saul's response to others who faced difficult or similar crises and yet trusted that God was working things out even if they couldn't see it. There's Abraham telling his son Isaac regarding the sacrifice that God "would provide." There's Moses at the Red Sea telling the people to stand and behold the glory of God. There was also Mary the mother of Jesus at the wedding banquet when the wine had run dry. It didn't appear that Jesus was going to do anything, but she said, "Just wait and see what he does." Though God may not do exactly what we thought He was going to do, or even when we thought He was going to do it, He is not indifferent to the hopes and needs of those who put their faith in Him.

It has been difficult to choose just one Bible character to illustrate how viewing God as indifferent affects our lives. I think it's because so many of us operate from the view of indifference many times throughout the day. If I were to be perfectly honest, I would have to admit that indifference is a tangle of lies about God that I still succumb to at times in my life. Whether it's the apostles in the boat asking Jesus, "Don't you care if we drown?" the pressure Saul feels because God has not provided the priest for the sacrifice, or Hagar, who in a time of trouble did not utter a single cry out to God after living in the house of Abraham, the "father of the faith" for years, indifference is a stronghold blocking many from experiencing God in fuller ways.

All of these situations reveal a problem that still arises today when God is viewed as indifferent. We may find ourselves in a desperate circumstance, or with the failed hope that God would have prevented a predicament altogether. The situation may be overwhelming, and we are hoping God will help us through, but it appears that he's going to be a no-show. Sometimes we just want something special for ourselves, but we think God would not be concerned with these desires that are not necessities. It doesn't matter whether these thoughts come from a victim mentality where one only asks for assistance in times of trouble, or from the mindset of a martyr who unconsciously is looking for the next heartache or a tragedy. If you struggle with this view of indifference, you are certainly not alone, and there is a way forward.

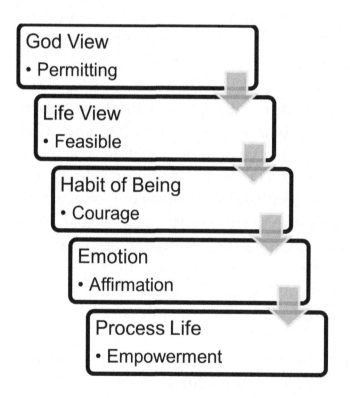

God View
• Permitting

Life View
• Feasible

Habit of Being
• Courage

Emotion
• Affirmation

Process Life
• Empowerment

Definition: Permit - to allow or grant.

"Jonathan said to his young armor-bearer, 'Come, let's go over to the outpost of those uncircumcised fellows. Perhaps the LORD will act in our behalf. Nothing can hinder the LORD from saving, whether by many or by few.' 'Do all that you have in mind,' his armor-bearer said."

1 Samuel 14:6-7

Jonathan and his young armor-bearer have launched out on their own initiative. They are not under direct orders. They were not assigned a specific task. Because Jonathan sees God as permitting the first among the positive and empowering views of God, his world is full of possibilities. Anything is feasible, even victory in the face of overwhelming odds.

When an idea comes to mind for Jonathan, there are no immediate thoughts that follow expressing how God would either not support the plan or would move actively against it. "Perhaps the Lord will act on our behalf" is a statement of belief. Jonathan sees God as one who wants him to explore and attempt the new and the bold. This view of God gives Jonathan the courage to step out and try his own ideas. Being successful in his efforts serves to affirm his faith and confidence that God is with him, that his ideas are valued, and his skills reliable.

On one occasion, Jonathan immediately countered his father's ill-conceived command for the men not to act until he "avenged himself." Jonathan's world is not one of self-doubt. He does not give deference to the thoughts of others merely because of their position. As a result, Jonathan and his young armor-bearer feel empowered to trust their ideas and strike out on their own initiative.

It's amazing what this first of the positive views of God unleashes in our lives. What could a person possess in their lives that would be of greater value than the strength, esteem, and energy that comes from knowing that God goes before you preparing the way? What would be intimidating knowing God is lowering mountains, raising valleys, removing obstacles, and clearing paths for the joy and progress of your life?

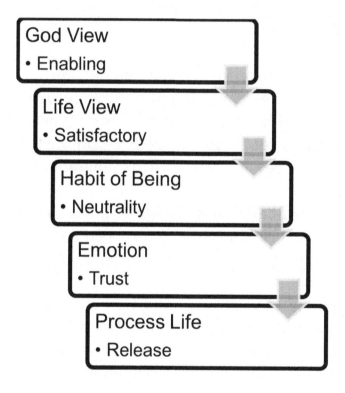

God View
• Enabling

Life View
• Satisfactory

Habit of Being
• Neutrality

Emotion
• Trust

Process Life
• Release

Definition: Enable - To render capable or able for some task; "This skill will enable you to find a job on Wall Street"; "The rope enables you to secure yourself when you climb the mountain."

Note: We are not using the word "enable" in the codependent sense, but rather the traditional meaning to empower.

"When word came to Sanballat, Tobiah, Geshem the Arab and the rest of our enemies that I had rebuilt the wall and not a gap was left in it—though up to that time I had not set the doors in the gates- Sanballat and Geshem sent me this message: 'Come, let us meet together in one of the villages on the plain of Ono.'

But they were scheming to harm me; so I sent messengers to them with this reply: 'I am carrying on a great project and cannot go down. Why should the work stop while I leave it and go down to you?' Four times they sent me the same message, and each time I gave them the same answer.

Then, the fifth time, Sanballat sent his aide to me with the same message, and in his hand was an unsealed letter in which was written:

'It is reported among the nations—and Geshem says it is true—that you and the Jews are plotting to revolt, and therefore you are building the wall. Moreover, according to these reports you are about to become their king and have even appointed prophets to make this proclamation about you in Jerusalem: There is a king in Judah! Now this report will get back to the king; so come, let us confer together.'

I sent him this reply: 'Nothing like what you are saying is happening; you are just making it up out of your head.'

They were all trying to frighten us, thinking, 'Their hands will get too weak for the work, and it will not be completed.'

But I prayed, 'Now strengthen my hands.'"

Nehemiah 6:1-9

Nehemiah makes it easy for us. It's clear from his prayer, "Now strengthen my hands," that Nehemiah views God as one who will enable him to take care of the needs and demands that come his way.

Despite how often Sanballat hurls his threats and twists the facts, Nehemiah remains unfazed by it all. There's a calmness with Nehemiah that I believe comes from his deep satisfaction with what God has revealed of Himself and how faithful He has been to all of His promises.

Life is not frustrating when you have the ability to meet its demands. For example, if we have a taste for a burger, you can reach into your pockets and find a $20 bill. There's no frustration. There's no angst. We're pretty satisfied. We want a burger, and we have the means to purchase a burger. All is good. If, however, we want a burger and reach into our pockets and find $0.35, we may experience a different set of emotions. Our level of satisfaction in life is tied to our deep sense of being able to meet its demands. Nehemiah does not complain that he shouldn't be in this situation. He doesn't go on and on about how things should or should not be. He has accepted the situation for what it is and prayed to his God to make a difference.

Though the odds seem to be stacked against him, Nehemiah is a model of trust. He neither runs, nor wallows in self-pity, nor charges God with neglect in the face of Sanballat's repeated assaults.

Nehemiah doesn't frantically scurry to make things happen. Like David recorded in the Psalms, Nehemiah has learned to "still and quiet his soul like a weaned child with its mother." He has released any preconditions he has on how life will be or how God must act. He is not tied to a particular outcome.

Of profound significance is the content of Nehemiah's prayer. He prays to his God to "now strengthen my hands."

Rather than pray that God changes the reality before him, Nehemiah prayed to be enabled, to be strengthened to successfully handle the reality in his life. Nehemiah is a great example to us of what it means to "lean in," rather than resist or avoid.

We often expend precious energy and indulge corrosive emotions wishing and hoping that reality was something other than it is. Acceptance is a powerful act Acceptance is what enables us to live in the moment. I'm reminded of the quote,

"It is not for us to know what lies dimly in the future, but to do what lies clearly at hand."

Thomas Carlyle

Nehemiah prayed for the strength to deal with what was clearly at hand. There's no discussion asking, "Why are there Sanballats in the world?" Nehemiah does not appear to be consumed with getting Sanballat to see things from his perspective, and that's what we mean by a habit of being of neutrality. Nehemiah does not need to polarize things. Life can go on quite satisfactorily without Sanballat ever agreeing with Nehemiah or coming to Nehemiah's view on things. Though this is beyond the scope of this book, this truth has profound implications for our relationships, whether they are friendships, marriages, parent-child, employer-employee, etc. There is a rich quality of life awaiting those who can maintain their neutrality and not always have to convince others or give up their own values under the pressure of others. Neutral people are safe to be around.

Is there any wonder why Nehemiah was able to garner such widespread support from among the people? Because of Nehemiah's contentment and neutrality, people felt safe to be themselves around him. They were even inspired to be the best version of themselves.

They completed the construction of the wall in just 52 days.

Accepting the enabling attributes of God at a heart level is a real game-changer.

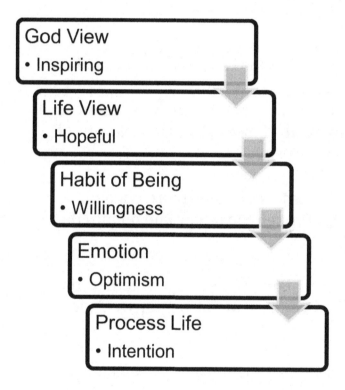

Definition: Inspire - arousing to a particular emotion or action

The LORD said to Moses,

"Send some men to explore the land of Canaan,

which I am giving to the Israelites. From each ancestral tribe send one of its leaders."

So at the LORD's command Moses sent them out from the Desert of Paran. All of them were leaders of the Israelites.

These are their names: from the tribe of Reuben, ...

from the tribe of Judah, Caleb son of Jephunneh...

These are the names of the men Moses sent to explore the land. (Moses gave Hoshea, son of Nun, the name Joshua.)

When Moses sent them to explore Canaan, he said, "Go up through the Negev and on into the hill country.

"See what the land is like and whether the people who live there are strong or weak, few or many.

"What kind of land do they live in? Is it good or bad? What kind of towns do they live in? Are they unwalled or fortified?

"How is the soil? Is it fertile or poor? Are there trees on it or not? Do your best to bring back some of the fruit of the land." (It was the season for the first ripe grapes.)

When they reached the Valley of Eshcol, they cut off a branch bearing a single cluster of grapes. Two of them carried it on a pole between them, along with some pomegranates and figs.

At the end of forty days, they returned from exploring the land.

They came back to Moses, Aaron, and the whole Israelite community at Kadesh in the Desert of Paran. There they reported to them and to the whole assembly and showed them the fruit of the land.

They gave Moses this account: "We went into the land to which you sent us, and it does flow with milk and honey! Here is its fruit.

"But the people who live there are powerful, and the cities are fortified and very large. We even saw descendants of Anak there.

"The Amalekites live in the Negev; the Hittites, Jebusites, and Amorites live in the hill country; and the Canaanites live near the sea and along the Jordan."

Then Caleb silenced the people before Moses and said, "We should go up and take possession of the land, for we can certainly do it."

But the men who had gone up with him said, "We can't attack those people; they are stronger than we are."

And they spread among the Israelites a bad report about the land they had explored. They said, "The land we explored devours those living in it. All the people we saw there are of great size... We seemed like grasshoppers in our own eyes, and we looked the same to them."

Numbers 13:1-33

That night all the people of the community raised their voices and wept aloud.

All the Israelites grumbled against Moses and Aaron, and the whole assembly said to them, "If only we had died in Egypt! Or in this desert!

Joshua, son of Nun, and Caleb, son of Jephunneh, who were among those who had explored the land, tore their clothes

and said to the entire Israelite assembly, "The land we passed through and explored is exceedingly good.

"If the LORD is pleased with us, He will lead us into that land, a land flowing with milk and honey, and will give it to us.

"Only do not rebel against the LORD. And do not be afraid of the people of the land, because we will swallow them up. Their protection is gone, but the LORD is with us. Do not be afraid of them."

But the whole assembly talked about stoning them. Then the glory of the LORD appeared at the Tent of Meeting to all the Israelites.

The LORD said to Moses, "...not one of them will ever see the land I promised on oath to their forefathers. No one who has treated me with contempt will ever see it.

"But because my servant Caleb has a different spirit and follows me wholeheartedly, I will bring him into the land he went to, and his descendants will inherit it."

Of the men who went to explore the land, only Joshua, son of Nun, and Caleb, son of Jephunneh, survived.

Now the men of Judah approached Joshua at Gilgal, and Caleb, son of Jephunneh the Kenizzite, said to him, "You know what the LORD said to Moses, the man of God at Kadesh Barnea about you and me.

"I was forty years old when Moses the servant of the LORD sent me from Kadesh Barnea to explore the land. And I brought him back a report according to my convictions, but my brothers who went up with me made the hearts of the people melt with fear. I, however, followed the LORD my God wholeheartedly.

"So on that day Moses swore to me, 'The land on which your feet have walked will be your inheritance and that of your children forever because you have followed the LORD my God wholeheartedly.'

"Now then, just as the LORD promised, he has kept me alive for forty-five years since the time he said this to Moses while Israel moved about in the desert. So here I am today, eighty-five years old!

I am still as strong today as the day Moses sent me out; I'm just as vigorous to go out to battle now as I was then.

Now give me this hill country that the LORD promised me that day. You yourself heard then that the Anakites were there and their cities were large and fortified, but, the LORD helping me, I will drive them out just as he said."

Then Joshua blessed Caleb son of Jephunneh and gave him Hebron as his inheritance.

So Hebron has belonged to Caleb son of Jephunneh

the Kenizzite ever since, because he followed the LORD, the God of Israel, wholeheartedly.

Numbers 14:1-45

The positive views of God we have looked at are permitting and enabling. Both of these center around the idea of God helping us to accomplish a particular desire. When it comes to viewing God as inspiring, here God takes the lead. He is the initiator of the thought or the desire. Now that we're convinced "all things are possible", we naturally begin to look among all possibilities for what is the best "thing" to pursue. This is where God enters our spiritual journey as a source of inspiration.

In Caleb's time, God had something better in mind for the Israelites than they were presently experiencing. God initiated the vision and the plan for Israel to leave Egyptian captivity and inherit the Promised Land. Caleb was inspired at the thought of such a future. Though he was not yet in physical possession of the Promised Land, Caleb had a hopeful outlook on life and his future.

Have you ever been in a situation when someone expressed a vision for your life that was grand but left you feeling more frustrated than hopeful? It's served as a reminder of what you did not have. It served only as a reminder of your present plight and failure to improve your position. It evoked a jealousy or envy of those already so blessed. No, the vision of a brighter future is not always met with hope.

But when one views God as inspiring, hope is renewed. After all, if God has inspired the idea who can "stay his hand" when he's decided to act, what are the chances of success or victory when God is behind something?

And so with success all but guaranteed, those who see God as inspiring are not only filled with hope, but find themselves willing participants in whatever is necessary to bring about the vision.

Caleb is willing to believe the vision of the Promised Land.

He is willing to scout out the land with the other leaders.

He is willing to express confidently what he saw and what he believed, even when it differed from the majority.

He is willing to go about pursuing the vision God's way.

He was willing to wait forty-five years.

He was willing to take on the most difficult assignment, the hill country.

This kind of willingness that Caleb demonstrates is hard to turn on just for critical moments. The willingness of which we speak must become a default disposition. This is a willingness that has become Caleb's habit of being. With Caleb, it was not a begrudging willingness. With him, there's always an optimism and a hope that whatever the moment required whether action or patience, it all led to the fulfillment of God's promise, the possession of the Promised Land.

Inner resistance and true willingness are incompatible with each other. Resistance has to do with protection and insisting on a particular approach: how we grew up, what our coaches taught, how our nationality or ethnic culture goes about things. Without resistance, we can wave hello to reality and acknowledge things as they actually are. In contrast, willingness shakes hands with how things truly are and enthusiastically says, "I'm in, let's work together." The willing build community, like Caleb. The unwilling criticize, don't engage and impede a community, family or organization's development.

Lastly, we see over the whole of Caleb's life a definiteness of purpose. Caleb is anything but haphazard. Caleb does not just happen to be a man of a "different spirit"; it is his intention to be this way. One cannot gain a reputation with God of "following him wholeheartedly" by chance. He had to make up his mind that he would meet every challenge with trust and faithfulness. He intends to believe God's promises. He chooses to believe that he will inherit the Promised Land even after waiting 45 years.

There were times as a parent when I had to address this issue with my children. After getting in trouble over something, it would not be uncommon for me to hear one of them say, "But I didn't intend to do that." To this, my response was always, "The problem is not that you didn't intend to do it. The problem is that you didn't intend not to do it."

When someone views God as inspiring, a lot of contemplation and "what if" scenarios take place in their thought process and planning. They anticipate specific results and outcomes that could occur which might appear as set-backs. With each possible outcome, they decide in advance the faithful attitude, course of action, and verbal expression (if any) with which they will respond should that possibility actually occur.

One of the best examples I can come up with is in the realm of sports. I've noticed a common response from players and coaches alike after last-second game-winning scores. Inevitably, the enthusiastic sports journalist will ask in the interview, "Could you even imagine coming back from such a deficit?" or, "Could you even imagine scoring from that distance with a half a second on the clock?" To these questions and others like them, the player or coach will look the journalist in the eye and say, "Yes, I could imagine it because we practiced that play every day." They had anticipated situations and agreed ahead of time what their mindset would be and what actions they would take. That kind of intention is not just the result of iron will or dogged determination; it is the fruit of inspiration.

For Caleb, God was inspiring.

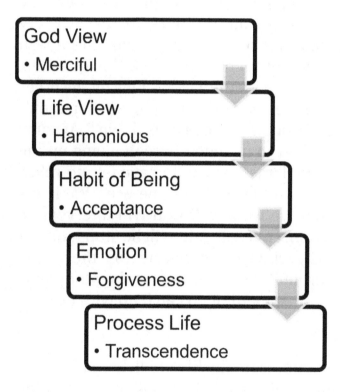

Definition: Mercy - is compassion or forgiveness shown toward someone whom it is within one's power to punish or harm.

We know that God forgives all our sin when we turn to Him and follow his plan of salvation. By His grace, we are saved and "put right with" Him. But will He intervene to withhold earthly consequences? Will He show mercy? How many times? Even after we know better? Let's look through Scripture to see why, when, and if God doesn't give some of us what we deserve.

Are the consequences removed or just suspended? It is like the Israelites on the shores of the Red Sea with Pharaoh's army in hot pursuit. God splits the Red Sea, giving a moment's relief from the pursuing army. Every person who crossed that sea on dry ground with a wall of water on each side of them had to ask this question, "Will he hold the waters back until I am safely on the other side?" and, "Even if we make it through, will Pharaoh's army cross the sea in boats and chase us down?" At some point, God's mercy had to include Pharaoh giving up the chase. Otherwise, the Israelites would have felt no relief, only a brief reprieve. Aren't we the same way? We know we are forgiven, but we wonder if God will intervene to stop some earthly consequence. And will he stop it or just delay it momentarily while we get our act together? How many of us walk around daily waiting for the other shoe to drop or waiting for something to catch up with us from the past?

Let's look at an account from the life of Elisha, a man who understood the mercy of God and how that understanding affected his outlook on life and how it unfolded around him.

> Now the king of Aram was at war with Israel. After conferring with his officers, he said, "I will set up my camp in such and such a place."

The man of God sent word to the king of Israel: "Beware of passing that place because the Arameans are going down there."

So the king of Israel checked on the place indicated by the man of God. Time and again Elisha warned the king so that he was on his guard in such places.

This enraged the king of Aram. He summoned his officers and demanded of them, "Will you not tell me which of us is on the side of the king of Israel?"

"None of us, my lord the king," said one of his officers, "but Elisha, the prophet who is in Israel, tells the king of Israel the very words you speak in your bedroom."

"Go, find out where he is," the king ordered, "so I can send men and capture him." The report came back: "He is in Dothan."

Then he sent horses and chariots and a strong force there. They went by night and surrounded the city.

When the servant of the man of God got up and went out early the next morning, an army with horses and chariots had surrounded the city. "Oh, my lord, what shall we do?" the servant asked.

"Don't be afraid," the prophet answered. "Those who are with us are more than those who are with them."

And Elisha prayed, "O LORD, open his eyes so he may see." Then the LORD opened the servant's eyes, and he looked and saw the hills full of horses and chariots of fire all around Elisha.

As the enemy came down toward him, Elisha prayed to the LORD, "Strike these people with blindness." So he struck them with blindness, as Elisha had asked.

Elisha told them, "This is not the road and this is not the city. Follow me, and I will lead you to the man you are looking for." And he led them to Samaria.

After they entered the city, Elisha said, "LORD, open the eyes of these men so they can see." Then the LORD opened their eyes and they looked, and there they were, inside Samaria.

When the king of Israel saw them, he asked Elisha, "Shall I kill them, my father? Shall I kill them?"

"Do not kill them," he answered. "Would you kill men you have captured with your own sword or bow? Set food and water before them so that they may eat and drink and then go back to their master."

So he prepared a great feast for them, and after they had finished eating and drinking, he sent them away, and they returned to their master. So the bands from Aram stopped raiding Israel's territory.

2 Kings 6:8-23

This story begins with an immediate contrast. Elisha is relaxed and at peace while his assistant is out of his mind with dread. Elisha makes obvious the difference between the two. He sees God as having already provided relief while his servant sees God as absent and uninvolved.

As the story unfolds, Elisha accepts it for what it is. Not all of God's prophets met life's events this way. Even Elijah, Elisha's mentor, was known to ask why his protection was gone when he had served God so faithfully. Elisha had the great benefit of seeing how graciously God dealt with his master. Despite the fears, complaints, and bouts of depression, God whisked Elijah to heaven in a glorious display of his pleasure with him. And Elisha saw it all. Elisha is able to accept with equanimity the things that life throws at him because he knows that not only will God make him adequate for the task, but that He will also cover his failings and work everything out to his good. God will even cover his sins and doubts, and intervene and work them out for Elisha's benefit. So Elisha can sing the refrain of one of my favorite church songs,

"Whatever's in front of me, I choose to sing hallelujah."

That is the cry of the heart that knows the mercy of God and accepts whatever his loving hand brings.

Mary, the mother of Jesus, expressed it this way when told by an angel that she would miraculously conceive and give birth to the son of God: "May it be to me as the Lord has spoken."

Part of acceptance is the understanding that God is sovereign and in control. Not a feather falls from a bird in the sky without it being the will of God. Acceptance is a pathway to forgiveness. One cannot be said to have accepted something and resent it at the same time. The acceptance-inspired forgiveness extends both to ourselves and others. When the king of Israel thought to kill his captured foes, Elisha thought to feed them, give them water, and send them unmolested back to their master. That is a model of mercy.

Elisha knows there is a reality beyond the material world. He has witnessed it, and he relies on it. That is what makes him transcendent. He is not limited by what he sees. Again, Elisha is a model for us of what it means to "live by faith and not by sight."

What a great hope Elisha extends to those of us who will embrace the mercy of God.

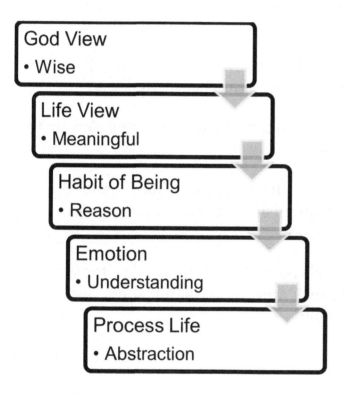

Definition: Wise - having or showing experience, knowledge, and good judgment.

When Joseph's brothers saw that their father was dead, they said, "What if Joseph holds a grudge against us and pays us back for all the wrongs we did to him?"

So they sent word to Joseph, saying, "Your father left these instructions before he died:

'This is what you are to say to Joseph: I ask you to forgive your brothers the sins and the wrongs they committed by treating you so badly.' Now please forgive the sins of the servants of the God of your father." When their message came to him, Joseph wept.

His brothers then came and threw themselves down before him. "We are your slaves," they said.

But Joseph said to them, "Don't be afraid. Am I in the place of God?

You intended to harm me, but God intended it for good to accomplish what is now being done, the saving of many lives.

So then, don't be afraid. I will provide for you and your children." And he reassured them and spoke kindly to them.

Genesis 50:15-21

Viktor Frankl, a survivor of the Holocaust, once said a man could put up with any "what" when there is a sufficient "why" behind it. Many people who entered the camps frailer than their neighbors outlived those seemingly healthier souls because they had a reason to live. There was someone back home who desperately needed them. They had a reason.

When we look at Joseph and the challenges he faced, we see he was able to maintain his heart, faith, and spirit because he knew that God was wise and that there was a reason and a purpose behind every event in his life. And they were not all for the purpose of teaching him a lesson or developing his character. In retrospect, Joseph could look back and connect the dots. However, while he was going through it, not knowing the ultimate outcome, he had to view each moment as being his destiny and not just a stepping stone to God's plan for his life.

Because Joseph saw God as wise, there was a reason to make the most of every station of his life. Abandonment by his brothers, slavery, false accusations and prison were his lot for 13 years. And yet Joseph found meaning in each and reasoned that each challenge merited his all and his best.

How often we find ourselves saying I just don't understand why a certain difficulty, conflict or problem is happening in our lives. And that lack of understanding becomes the foundation of a world of anxiety and frustration. There were times in my life when disappointments and setbacks would take place, and I could meet them with a faith and trust that God was working it out for some grand scheme. But after a "series of unfortunate events," something changed. I began to conclude that who I was and what I had to offer was no longer valued in my community. I came to believe that you can always change how you approach an issue or settle a matter, but you cannot change the essence of who you are. Unbeknownst to me, I was drifting into a questioning of why God made me as He did. I was unconsciously questioning why He gave me the experiences He did. Why He was forming me and shaping me to hold the convictions that I did. In short, for many years, the values I held so dearly seemed to be of no interest to the people of influence around me. No one seemed to be interested in what I had to offer.

It is interesting to look at God's perspective on what is taking place in Joseph's life. God gave Joseph a vision of greatness that made his brothers hate him and sell him into slavery. Still God was with him and gave him success in whatever he did. He did such a great job relating to his master's wife that she accused him of attempted rape and his master put him in prison. Still God was with him and gave him success in whatever he did. He left such a lasting impression on his fellow inmates that when they were released from prison, they forgot about him for two years while he remained behind. Again, God was with him and gave him success in whatever he did. All this is to say that Joseph very well could have asked, if God is with me why has he not given me success with my brothers, success with my master's wife and success with my fellow inmates? We are not privy to much of what Joseph thought in prison, but we do have this comment he made to the cupbearer when he learned he was to be released. Joseph said:

> "This is what it means," Joseph said to him. "The three branches are three days.

> Within three days Pharaoh will lift up your head and restore you to your position, and you

will put Pharaoh's cup in his hand, just as you used to do when you were his cupbearer.

But when all goes well with you, remember me and show me kindness; mention me to Pharaoh and get me out of this prison.

For I was forcibly carried off from the land of the Hebrews, and even here I have done nothing to deserve being put in a dungeon."

Genesis 40:12-15

From these comments, it does not appear that Joseph believed he did anything wrong or was responsible in any way for being forcibly removed from his homeland or put in prison. But neither does he blame his father for bad parenting, his brothers for jealousy, his master's wife for lying, or the Egyptian justice system for corruption. Things just are as they are. But that doesn't mean he doesn't greatly desire that his situation changes. Without self-pity, resentment, assigning blame or vengeance, Joseph is emotionally free, spiritually connected and physically unencumbered by the stress of anger or the drain of depression. He is free to make the most of whatever situation in which he finds himself. Joseph's trust in the wisdom of God keeps the debilitating task of justifying himself and manipulating every event to his advantage off of his shoulders. He has not resigned himself to fate or chance, and his life and times are firmly in the hands of a wise and loving God who intends him good.

We're not saying here that Joseph was devoid of any emotions over this period of his life, but we see that he can let reason drive his actions rather than emotion. By reason, Joseph is able to continue moving forward long before he is given the place of honor next to Pharaoh. By reason, Joseph is able to work out complicated issues like the sovereignty of God, the presence of evil in the world, destiny, individual freedom, famine, God's promise that his children would never go hungry, slavery, a broken criminal justice system, and many other seemingly contradictory realities into a seamless tapestry woven by God.

His dominant emotion is one of understanding. At the critical moment with all of his brothers present, those very men whose actions triggered years of unjust treatment for Joseph, Joseph possessed full authority to do with them whatever he wished. It is neither resentment nor retaliation but rather understanding that emerges as Joseph's driving emotion. With his brothers pleading for their lives, what's most important to Joseph is that they comprehend what he has come to understand. There is a great and loving God, who has worked all these things out to bring about the salvation of many people, a God so wise that he could use the sin and folly of a family of young men to save that same family from perishing.

Joseph explained to his brother that there was a reason that all of these seemingly tragic events had taken place. A wise and all-knowing God had worked through these circumstances to amass life-saving provisions for millions of people.

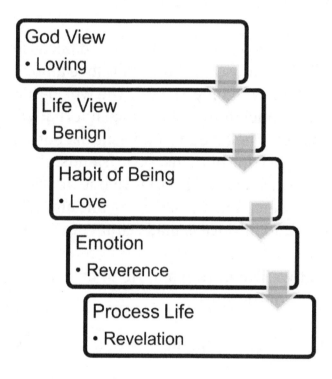

God View
• Loving

Life View
• Benign

Habit of Being
• Love

Emotion
• Reverence

Process Life
• Revelation

Definition: Loving - an unconditional longing for and commitment to the well-being of another that is pure, free of personal agenda, unfailing, constant, and unaffected by external circumstances.

Though abundant examples fill our world, this kind of love

is rarely reported on the nightly news. It is not the topic of water cooler discussions at work. As a result, I feel the need to spend more time with this view of God than any of the others. We can never fill our minds with too many images that reflect God's love and give us a fighting chance of seeing him as he actually is.

John, the Apostle of love, writes the following:

> Whoever does not love does not know God because God is love. This is how God showed his love among us: He sent his one and only Son into the world that we might live through him. This is love: not that we loved God, but that he loved us and sent his Son as an atoning sacrifice for our sins. Dear friends, since God so loved us, we also ought to love one another. No one has ever seen God; but if we love one another, God lives in us and his love is made complete in us.
>
> We know that we live in Him and He in us because He has given us of His Spirit.
>
> And so we know and rely on the love God has for us.
>
> God is love. Whoever lives in love lives in God, and God in him. In this way, love is made complete among us so that we will have confidence on the Day of Judgment because in this world we are like him. There is no fear in love. But perfect love drives out fear because fear has to do with punishment. The one who fears is not made perfect in love.

We love because he first loved us. If anyone says, "I love God," yet hates his brother, he is a liar. For anyone who does not love his brother, whom he has seen, cannot love God, whom he has not seen. And he has given us this command: Whoever loves God must also love his brother.

1 John 4:8-21

John is obviously one of those fortunate souls who see God as loving. For these people, life is benign. It is not characterized by threat, danger, harm, injury, and fear. The good, peaceful, harmonious, and cooperative aspects of life outnumber the occasions of strife by a thousand fold. Life is an immense cooperative whole. There is a harmony in life. There is a oneness where differences are seen as aspects of a whole instead of evidence of separateness.

John, who sees God as love, finds himself loving others in response. John speaks of love more frequently than any other writer in scripture. For John, love became the message of Jesus and the answer to all problems between people. To say that love had become John's habit of being would be an understatement. Love now tempers John. He exudes an attitude of love. His leadership style could be described as kindness and love. Like John, those who truly grasp the loving nature of God increasingly make love toward all their general way of being. Their feelings toward others are not indifferent or hostile but rather a specialness, sacredness, and reverence. This reverence is not an act of worship but a recognition of the spark of God in every living thing.

Look at the Apostle John. In his life, he moves from being considered one of the Sons of Thunder to being known as the Apostle of love. People are no longer viewed as obstinate obstacles to the will of God but rather as beloved children of the Father.

John says we love because he first loved us. When we don't perceive God as loving, we are not moved from within to love in the manner for which we were created.

The life process for one who beholds and views God as love is described as a revelation. Again, it will be helpful to explain what we don't mean by revelation. We're not talking about hearing a voice from God telling us to write the next chapter of the Bible. No, we're talking about a revelation where a person sees the evidence of God at work day by day. By revelation, we mean insights that are given in matters well beyond the amount of information a person has on the topic. These insights are merely discernment of the Spirit's promptings and guidance in our lives.

It's not that we need to ascend to heights of seeing God as loving for Him to speak to us. God is speaking and communicating to all of us all the time. It's just that the limiting and inaccurate views of God come with a lot of noise and clutter that can drown out God's voice. Should we happen to hear what he says, any negative view of God would make us far less inclined to believe that His instructions to us are actually for our benefit.

The Apostle John seems to have overcome a lot of personal inclination, family and cultural upbringing, and political and environmental circumstances. Through the overwhelming influence of believing the words of Jesus, John came to see God as he truly is: a God of love.

Chapter Twenty – One - Jesus

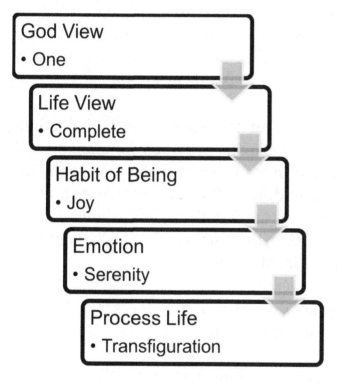

God View
- One

Life View
- Complete

Habit of Being
- Joy

Emotion
- Serenity

Process Life
- Transfiguration

Definition: One - being the same in kind or quality; 1) constituting a unified entity of two or more components; 2) being in agreement or union, i.e. I am one with you on this.

How did Jesus view God? In addition to dying on the cross to pay the penalty of our sins, a major part of Jesus' mission on Earth was to "reveal the Father." Another way of saying this is that Jesus came to make known truths about God that may not be grasped by observing creation or having a detailed knowledge of the Scriptures. One of the greatest blessings of our lives would be the ability to embrace the truth about God as Jesus revealed and saw Him.

First of all, Jesus most often referred to God as the Father. In his prayers, he used the adjective "Abba" in front of the word father. This was an endearing sentiment reflecting how small children addressed their fathers. Not so much as Dad or Pops, but closer to Daddy or Poppa.

There was tenderness in the expression Abba father. Jesus viewed God as the loving provider, companion, and guide who delighted in every stage of his development. Even when Jesus found himself at the receiving end of a venomous tirade from a hostile crowd, he responded with an astonishing assertion. He announced, "The Father loves the Son and shows him all he does."

Jesus went beyond declaring God's loves for him to proclaiming that he was one with God.

"I and the Father are one." (John 10:30)

He longed for the apostles to understand this truth. In an encounter recorded in John 14, Jesus was perplexed that the 12 apostles still had not fully grasped who he was.

"Philip said, 'Lord, show us the Father and that will be enough for us.'

Jesus answered: 'Don't you know me, Philip, even after I have been among you such a long time? Anyone who has seen me has seen the Father'... 'The words I say to you I do not speak on my own authority. Rather, it is the Father, living in me, who is doing his work. Believe me when I say that I am in the Father and the Father is in me."

John 14:8-10

Jesus' claim to be one with God was a challenge for his followers to understand fully and was considered irreverent heresy to his detractors. That same tension fills the air whenever a believer asserts their kinship with God. Often, any comments we make about being a part of God still invites hostility from some. But the truth is the truth. When it comes to the believer, "You are of Christ and Christ is of God" (1 Corinthians 3:23). We are in Jesus, and Jesus is in the Father. However you want to slice it, we have been made part of the divine family. Remember the promise of Ephesians 3 that we would be filled to the measure with all the fullness of Christ? We are not God, but God invites us to be one with Him.

As for how Jesus viewed life, little could compare. Jesus came to the world, ministered to the lost, and suffered death on a cross that we might have life. He even gave his best and his all that we would live life to the fullest.

Have you ever thought to yourself, "Did Jesus sacrifice to give me the quality of life I'm living?" or, "Wouldn't the life of the Son of God purchase for me something better than

I'm presently experiencing?"

Jesus saw life as complete. Nothing was lacking in his relationship with the Father. He was in complete harmony with God: "whatever the Father does, the son also does." Jesus knew he had come from God and was returning to God. In John 17, he declared that he had, "...brought you (God) glory on earth by finishing the work you gave me to do."

Jesus met every day literally with "the joy of the Lord." It was a gift he wanted the Apostles to possess. Upon admonishing his twelve closest disciples to remain faithful, he said,

"I have told you this so that my joy may be in you and that your joy may be complete. My command is this: Love each other as I have loved you."

John 15:11-13

I have always been impressed with the composure of Jesus. He quietly wrote on the ground while an angry crowd threatened to stone a woman he was protecting. He walked right through a mob that was trying to throw him off a cliff. He confidently proclaimed the life-giving power of God while the townspeople wailed in grief at the death of Lazarus.

Transfiguration has been described as "a complete change of form or appearance into a more beautiful or spiritual state."

Jesus was the epitome of transformation.

"After six days Jesus took with him Peter, James, and John the brother of James, and led them up a high mountain by themselves. There he was transfigured before them. His face shone like the sun, and his clothes became as white as the light. Just then there appeared before them Moses and Elijah, talking with Jesus."

Matthew 17:1-3

The central message and controversy of the Gospel center around Jesus' oneness with God. A conflict Jesus had with the crowd in John 5 makes the point:

"Why then do you accuse me of blasphemy because I said, 'I am God's Son'? Do not believe me unless I do the works of my Father. But if I do them, even though you do not believe me, believe the works, that you may know and understand that the Father is in me, and I in the Father. Again they tried to seize him, but he escaped their grasp."

John 10:36-39

CHAPTER TWENTY-ONE
A MATTER OF PERSPECTIVE

"It has well been said that we do not see things as they are, but as we are ourselves. Everyman looks through the eyes of his prejudices, of his preconceived notions. Hence, it is the most difficult thing in the world to broaden a man so that he will realize truth as other men see it."

Dean Samuel Silas Curry

Harvard 1891

As we have seen, the Bible is full of characters and demonstrations of how our view of God has a powerful influence on how our life unfolds. The natural question is why we don't just see God as loving and let the blessings begin. The truth of the matter is we 1) view our world through distorted lens, and 2) look in the wrong places. We all see God and everything else through a particular lens or point of view.

No matter how hard we squint, even the most beautiful image will be distorted by a faulty lens.

You'll notice when we visit the optometrist to get our eyes examined if we can't read what's on the chart the doctor never prescribes a corrected image; he or she prescribes a corrective lens.

Jesus put it this way: "The eye is the lamp of the body. If your eyes are healthy, your whole body will be full of light. But if your eyes are unhealthy, your whole body will be full of darkness. If then the light within you is darkness, how great is that darkness!" Matthew 6:2-23.

Notice that Jesus does not call the eye a window, a mere pane of glass where the light just passes through. He compares the eye to a lamp, the very source of light. It is the source of the image that is projected onto the screen of our minds.

The actual lens in our eyes is made up of physical material. But the lens that Jesus is speaking of is not our physical eye. It's not made up of physical components. This spiritual eye is made up of the point of view from which we observe life and the agreements or conclusions we have drawn from the events that have taken place in our lives. The work involved in correcting our spiritual vision centers around identifying our point of view in any given moment and dismantling the agreements that dictate our attitudes, emotions, and actions.

It is in our minds that we create the portraits of who we think we are. Sometimes we see ourselves with positive features, while at other times, they are not so positive.

The important truth to keep in mind is that none of these images are accurate representations of who we really are. They are, at best, mental constructs we assemble with the thoughts of the moment and conclusions we draw based on our personal history.

We experience a profound leap in clarity, a real "aha" moment when we come to understand we are not the mental constructs we have created.

These mental constructs sometimes take on personas of their own. We create personas for different situations in life, relationships, business, threats, etc. The problem arises when all of these personas get mistaken for our true identity, speak for us, and gang up to exacerbate difficult situations.

We greatly increase our chance of correcting our spiritual vision when we acknowledge our spiritual vision is not 20/20.

Where we habitually focus has a tremendous influence on our ability to see God for his many attributes of love as well.

The moon is only 1/400 the size of the sun. Even with its small size, when positioned just so, it can almost completely block any sight of the sun. Likewise, many of the things we focus on and to which we let our attention gravitate, prevent us from recognizing the evidence of God's loving nature. As we let our focus on one irritant give way to the next frustration, any sight of God's love is eclipsed over the course of an entire day or even longer.

Many of us have seen the social experiments that show how focusing on a particular subject can blind us to other things right in front of us. My favorite is the experiment where people are told to count the number of times dancers on the stage move in and out of a circle on the floor. The overwhelming majority of participants in the experiments completely miss the woman dressed up in a bear costume who dances from one side of the stage to the other.

The Apostle Paul says to "set your mind on things above." The first step to setting your mind is to set what you are mainly pursuing. Whatever we are primarily trying to accomplish, that very thing, and things like it, will naturally be in our minds. It would be difficult to set our minds on cooking if our chief aim in life was to be a professional baseball player. If baseball is the goal, then the "things of baseball" will dominate our thoughts.

When you think about the rest of this day, above all else, what must you get done? Do you have a deadline to meet? Is there a quota or numeric target you must reach? Too often we forfeit the hope of true, noble and pure thoughts by allowing "lesser things" to be the dominating aim of the day.

The mind is never idle. It is always occupied with something. Given this, it requires effort to feed the mind constantly with wholesome things. The mind is like a garden. If left unattended and uncultivated, weeds will grow all by themselves. You don't need to plant weeds. They need no watering. You don't have to protect them from frost or tie them to a stick for support when they are young and tender. They just grow.

Isn't that the way it is with thoughts? They just appear, uninvited, with seemingly no effort at all from us. These "weed" thoughts are usually wayward, useless and distracting at best. It takes great effort and divine assistance to bring to mind faithful and ennobling thoughts. This work to cultivate the garden of our thoughts is the central work of our mortal lives. As a matter of fact, when asked, "What is the work that God would have us do?" Jesus replied, "The work of God is this, to believe in the one he has sent."

The work is to believe. There are many metaphors in scripture for how challenging this work is. It is like resisting high winds and rising waters. It's like uprooting a tree, or tearing down a fort. Like defending your home from a strong man, it's hard.

It's embarrassing to me when I consider how many years I have foolishly wished to wake up with my mind filled to the brim with all the inspiring and courageous acts of God and people I've studied over the years. But I don't wake up this way. It is work for me to call these things to mind. Each morning requires a conscious effort to call to mind the truth that sets me free, the truth that transforms my being, the truth that creates righteous desires within me and spurs me on to "love and good deeds." This childish obsession with how things "should be" has caused me much trouble over the years. I have railed and raged, "I shouldn't have to be reminded and I shouldn't have to reread these great truths every morning." Can't I just wake up happy, energized, and full of faith and enthusiasm?

Apparently not. I have felt guilty over this, depressed about it. I have envied those who seem to wake and bounce out of bed with youthful exuberance. But when I begin to compare myself with some soul who appears to have an easier time of things, the words of Jesus to Peter come to mind: "What if [John] remains alive until I return? What is that to you? You must follow me." So, I have laid down my arms and given up this fight. My garden, unattended, grows weeds all day and every night. I must tend to it, first thing, every morning and throughout the entire day. This is what it means to "fight the good fight of the faith," to "above all else guard your heart, for it is the wellspring of life."

Whether it's first thing in the morning or through the many moments of the day, the first things we need to do to get our hearts and minds and souls in a place to hear the word of God is to acknowledge that He is the source of truth. That practically means we will have to take captive every thought and make it obedient to the truth as God has revealed it. I was talking to my wife, Lauri, the other day, confessing and acknowledging the challenge of writing this book. One of the greatest challenges is the desire to live out the truths I've referenced. I know

I fall short of implementing everything all the time, and it makes me hesitant to encourage others to take a path I haven't mastered. I told her how challenging it is feeling the difference between where I am spiritually at the moment and where I'd like to be. It would seem to be as simple as giving up a certain thought pattern and embracing the truth. Such a switch in thought would take a second of time and require less than a calorie of energy. However, thinking differently can still feel like a mountain to scale. As I spoke with Lauri, a term came to mind that best describes the challenge: "emotional indulgence."

We can become so accustomed to feeling a certain way and going down a certain line of thought that it's as though we belong there, and the path is smooth and level, or maybe even a little bit greased and with a downhill slant. The difficulty is not in knowing what to think, nor is the difficulty in beginning the first accurate thought that leads to other true thoughts.

The challenge is in moving from a familiar, predictable thought to a less familiar, less initially comfortable truth. It is a form of sensual indulgence that must be denied to make the leap. A leap is probably not the best way to describe it, but rather a small step requiring little energy. However, it is new, and it is different. That emotional indulgence is also a not-so-subtle form of justification. In other words, as long as we hold on to the untrue thoughts that take us to unspiritual places, we have an explanation for why our light is not shining, and our circumstances are not more reflective of a godly or Christ-focused life.

So armed with the knowledge of what's been holding us back, we can begin a brand new journey, from one nerve connection to the next. Though the process of choosing different thoughts may require less than a calorie of energy, we know at times we are inadequate to the task, but with God all things are possible.

CHAPTER TWENTY-TWO
I CAN SEE CLEARLY NOW

"Once more Jesus put his hands on the man's eyes. Then his eyes were opened, his sight was restored, and he saw everything clearly."

Mark 8:25

"The real voyage of discovery consists not in seeking new landscapes but in having new eyes."

Marcel Proust

Just how do we go about bringing clarity to our vision of God? We learn how to shift our perspective. We also come to understand the process of how debilitating agreements are dissolved and rendered powerless in our lives. Lastly, we come to a deeper knowledge of the truths that radically change our lives.

This is intense territory for most of us. The realization that we have views of God which are not accurate or even biblical can be disturbing. It is not uncommon for people to get down on, criticize, and condemn themselves for having such thoughts. They can come to see themselves as "unspiritual." Frustration, angst, and self-judgement will only hinder our efforts here. Self-criticism is not conducive to bringing about the kind of changes we desire.

Jesus put it this way: "Man's anger does not bring about the righteous life that God desires." (James 1:20)

Also, consider this Old Testament admonition:

"In quietness and in confidence shall be your strength."

Isaiah 30:15

The passage above reveals to us that spiritual strength comes through being quiet and confident, not agitated and condemned. The scriptures seem to tell us that there is more power in quietness and trust than angry resistance. Many in the social sciences call this dynamic "acceptance."

By acceptance, they mean a willingness to acknowledge that things are as they are. It is the absence of an assertion of how things should be or ought to be. By acceptance, we do not mean that we agree with the situation, just that we fully acknowledge the reality of the situation. After all, doesn't "best practices" problem-solving begin with clearly defining the problem?

The opposite of acceptance is referred to as "resistance." It's hard to be in active resistance and maintain a spirit of quietness and trust at the same time. Quietness and trust require acceptance.

When we accept ourselves, others, and life as they are, we stop burning precious energy arguing about how they ought to be. We are no longer blinded by the image of how something should be. We are clear to see the beauty of what lies before us. We are not blinded to the opportunities, resources and wisdom around us that can help bring about the desired change.

The life and ministry of Jesus is a model of acceptance.

- He was born to an unwed mother

- His country was under Roman occupation

- Gangs and bandits roamed the streets

- Insurrectionists had gathered to overthrow the Roman government

- The local governor was murderously corrupt

- The poor, blind, and the homeless begged on the road sides

- His religion was splintered into factions

- His brothers doubted his true identity

- His best friends deserted him in his hour of greatest need.

Despite all of the above, the scriptures are curiously absent of any statements by Jesus that life shouldn't be this way. On the contrary, regarding wars and uprisings, Jesus said, "These things must happen." Regarding the poor, Jesus said, "You will always have the poor with you."

Jesus stood on an unshakable foundation of acceptance, combined with an irrepressible passion for what could be.

This attitude of acceptance was a common trait in the lives of many Old Testament heroes.

Job addresses the issue directly in speaking to his disgruntled wife:

"He replied, 'You are talking like a foolish woman. Shall we accept good from God, and not trouble?'"

Job 2:9

Others modeled acceptance in their life choices and relationships.

In Genesis 13, instead of arguing with Lot's servants over which land to settle in, Abraham accepted the lesser quality parcels.

His son Isaac followed his example. In Genesis 26 he chose to give up the wells that had been dug by his servants rather than argue over them with the herdsmen of Gerar.

In Genesis 45, Joseph overlooked the abuse he had taken from his brothers. He didn't inflict punishment on them but rejoiced in their reunion instead.

Acceptance doesn't mean giving in; acceptance means getting ready!

There is much angst in believing that God's will, truth, and reality are somehow different than what you are experiencing. To think that the truth involves some "ought to be" or "should be" is off track. Rather the day is well begun with the thought:

> So Lord, it is from this place that you have ordained that I know and understand that YOU are working everything out for my good, my joy, and my progress in the faith.

So from here on out, no resistance, no pushing back. Lean in!

Further still regarding acceptance, one of the most empowering realities we can come to acknowledge is that other people do not cause most of the problems in our lives. Our problems are not "out there." The overwhelming majority of our persistent challenges can be directly attributed to arguing with reality instead of embracing truth and taking actions that can improve our condition.

Consider these observations from Byron Katie, the author of the book, *Loving What Is.*

"When I argue with reality, I lose—but only 100%

"What's happening is happening, and no amount of wishing on your end is going to make it any different at that moment. So, why not take a deep breath and reflect on the following: "How do I know that the wind should blow? It's blowing!"

"The only time we suffer is when we believe a thought that argues with what is. When the mind is perfectly clear, what is, is what we want."

"If you want to argue with what is, you will suffer. In fact, if you want reality to be different than what it is, you might as well try to teach a cat to bark."

"Everything happens for me, not to me." And, "Until you can see everything in the world as your friend, your work is not done."

"If I think that someone else is causing my problem, I'm insane."

"If I had a prayer, it would be this: 'God, spare me from the desire for love, approval, or appreciation. Amen.'"

"As you inquire into issues and turn judgments around, you come to see that every perceived problem appearing 'out there' is nothing more than a misperception within your own thinking."

Accepting that we don't have control over others or what is going to happen is the last element of acknowledging reality that we will address. Beware! This illusion of control is a deeply embedded fantasy in most of us. We try to control relationships, the behavior of others, and our children. Don't be surprised if it takes awhile to dig this splinter out of your mind.

Byron Katie states it succinctly below:

"I can find only three kinds of business in the universe: mine, yours and God's. Much of our stress comes from mentally living out of our business."

"God's business: Why would we think we should be able to control an earthquake or a flood?"

Now that we have established a foundation of acceptance, let's begin looking further into our strategies for seeing God clearly.

We are about to learn how to stop gravitating toward erroneous views of God and turn our attention to the truth.

As we discussed in the introduction, the precise nature of our inaccurate impressions is elusive. What we really believe about God can hide behind years of religious rhetoric. Our strategy then is to identify a slightly less elusive element, our dominant emotions, and work from there. Recall that a dominant emotion is the feeling within us that is most prevalent throughout the day. It is the emotion that stays with us the longest and returns more frequently than all the other emotions.

"Most of the time I feel ____."

Our emotions play a necessary and vital role in our spiritual lives. They are great indicators of how aligned or misaligned our thoughts and actions are from what we value most and universal truths. In this way, emotions can serve as a Guidance System.

Our five senses register and interpret vibrations and frequencies of all sorts from the environment. We are most conscious of the stimuli that relate closest to the object(s) of our attention, but unpleasant and disturbing emotions will indicate a contradiction to some value or agreement at a subconscious level.

They give an accurate reading of how aligned or misaligned our focus is with respect to the true nature of God and our relation to him. Babies are blissful, at least in part, because there are no contradictions within them. They have no thoughts or interpretations that run contrary to what they are experiencing. Perhaps the intensity of their cries at times reflects their anger and resentment toward anything like gas or hunger that disturbs their bliss. DON'T DISTURB THIS GROOVE!

Many of us may enjoy a similar peace when out in nature. Who looks at a sunset and says, "These colors are all wrong?" Who strolls through a forest and stands in judgment over the arrangement of the trees?

Therefore, Jesus tells us that unless we change and become like little children, we will in no way enter the kingdom of God, so it's back to the manger if we want to go forward with God.

Over the course of our lives, we come to hold many things to be true. Some of these beliefs are contrary to each other. Our emotions can signal which of these truths are the object of our present focus or what we most hold to be true. Once we identify our dominant emotion, there are just a few steps required to unraveling the thoughts and impressions that drive those emotions and make up our view of God.

It is our dominant thought that wins, rules, and reveals the day. This is our core belief. To this, Jesus said,

"'...it will be done just as you believed it would.' 'According to your faith will it be unto you.' The eye is the lamp of the body. If the light within is good, your whole body will be full of light. But if the light within is darkness how great is that darkness."

Matthew 6:22-23

The eye that Jesus spoke of was not the physical eye that receives the light of the physical world, but the spiritual eye. It is this "eye" that projects interpretation of our experiences and observations along with our conclusions about God's involvement, lack of involvement and intent regarding our lives.

We can use our emotions to feel our way back to well-being, wholeness, holiness, blessedness, bliss.

Start by identifying your dominant emotion mentioned in Chapter 5. Locate that emotion on the "Views of God" table. From there, move left past the "Habit of Being" and the "Life View" to the associated "God View."

If that view of God is anything less than "inspiring," we have work to do. Remember, we see God in erroneous and negative ways because of painful emotions, unsettling memories, and unconscious commitments. Sound familiar? That's right, it's our old friend, agreements.

Again, what do we mean by agreements? And how do they form? Maybe I can best explain agreements with a little exercise.

Imagine yourself traveling to a city for the first time. On the highway, you see your exit in the distance. As you approach the exit ramp, you notice it is landscaped beautifully, like a garden. You think to yourself, "Well, it looks like appearance is important to this city." The main street on the way to your hotel is nicely paved and smooth. As you pull up to the hotel, you notice free self-parking conveniently located just to the right of the entrance. As you approach the entrance, you are warmly greeted at the door. The young man at the desk has already pulled your reservation and prepared your room keycard in anticipation of your arrival. The next day, you enjoy a delicious complimentary breakfast. Your event goes off without a hitch, and your return flight arrives at the gate 15 minutes early.

That's the exercise. On an unconscious level, you may make an agreement something like this: "I like that city," "It's beautiful, well kept, and the people are nice," "I'd like to go back again sometime," or, "The business community is friendly and open to new ideas."

That's an agreement. It's the emotion, meaning, images, and decisions we make on an unconscious level regarding how we will respond the next time a similar event takes place. We make agreements like this about thousands of events in our lives on a subconscious basis.

We have agreements about places, people, the weather, sports teams, food, school, fitness, and fashion. You name it; if we've experienced anything in our lives, we likely have an agreement about it. These agreements and combinations of agreements compete with our intellectual understanding of life, and most importantly, with who God really is.

Agreements are formed and held together by the confidence we place in the evidence we use to form our opinions. We draw conclusions about what an event means and how we will react in similar circumstances next time. At the moment, it all feels logical.

Now that we know how agreements work, we can set about how to dismantle the ones that harm our relationship with God. We begin the process to disarm these agreements by resolving to set our minds on the true attributes of God. While we take the time to allow the process to have its effect, we'll have to accept that for a while, these agreements will continue to pose a bit of a challenge. The good thing about agreements is that the confidence which holds them together is easily dissolved when the shaky credibility of the evidence is exposed.

In reality, when agreements are formed, we are aware of only a fraction of the facts that surrounded the situation. That's because we experience most things in our lives from a particular vantage point. That perspective is highly influenced by groups of interrelated agreements.

Perspectives are powerful. When an expert in the law stood up to test Jesus and asked him, "What must I do to inherit eternal life?" Jesus responded, "What is written in the Law?" "How do you read it?"

Jesus understands better than anyone how we see things from a particular point of view.

We all have our own perspective, and that perspective has been created based on our upbringing, parents, culture, temperament, etc. My perspective and your perspective are made up of clusters of agreements. Each cluster is tailor-made to help us respond to different situations.

Earlier we looked at Bible characters that represented archetypes from the different views of God. Now we will look at a handful of archetypes that help us identify attributes of our own perspectives. These are the perspectives that create the most upheaval in our lives. Check out the following troublemakers and see if any of them sound familiar:

(1) The Judge. The Judge is always comparing. His primary role is to compare and choose a side. On any given subject the Judge will determine whether we are worse than or better than someone else. The Judge compares appearance, weight, intelligence, strength, wealth, position, popularity, etc. If we are deemed better, our self-worth rises. If we are judged as worse than, then it plummets. The Judge even renders decisions on how we perform based on an imaginary version of ourselves. We can condemn ourselves for failing to live up to an image of perfection. The Judge also condemns or acquits other people, the world, the government, and nature, for not meeting some imagined standard that doesn't exist in reality as well.

(2) The Victim. The victim archetype comes from the perspective that the world has done them wrong, that there's no hope, and that it's powerless to affect positive change in this life. It may conclude, "Why even try? The odds are stacked against me." The Victim believes, "I don't deserve this." "The man" has conspired and is out to get you. There is little safety, a lot of fear, and perpetual blame shifting with the Victim.

(3) The Hero. The Hero has to make everything right or ok. The Hero's primary motivation for rushing in and making things ok is to protect and save themselves or others from harm. He/she also tries to prove themselves worthy by good deeds. This is a plea for appreciation, reward, attention, respect or acceptance. The Hero places us on a performance treadmill, ever in need of winning the praise and affection of onlookers by some outstanding task performed. There is a sincere motivation for helping others. With the Hero, however, the selfless motivation is laced with self-promotion over the well-being of another.

(4) The Saboteur. The Saboteur works with a person's diminished self-image. This person feels like they only deserve so much. If a person prospers beyond their self-image, the Saboteur will find a way for the person to fail or suffer some loss until their level of prosperity is brought down to a level commensurate with their sense of personal value. The loss may be personal, relational, financial, emotional, or physical.

That Saboteur will respond to events or perceived slights in a disproportional manner. The overreaction can be an unconscious way of sabotaging a relationship or opportunity for which the person does not feel worthy. The actions of the Saboteur may be direct or through neglect. The end result would be the same, loss.

(5) The King. The King archetype is always interested in getting their way. Their mindset is, "people ought to do what I say." And if others don't comply, the King spews

anger, frustration, slander, etc. Its basic position is that the King's thoughts and opinions should hold sway over all others.

The King is always right, makes the rules and will not be second-guessed. His authority, position, size, etc. is used to shut down any opposition. The King may be a great dad, or boss, or partner, providing for others, but at the same time still have the attitude of a tyrant. Wisdom may prevent the King from always expressing his resentment or rage. Though outwardly civil, inside the King may harbor hostility and ill-will toward others.

(6) The Martyr - The attitude of the martyr is that he/she is to suffer the loss of pleasure, good things, hopes, and dreams so he/she can prove how devoted they are. This person will find a way to suffer, a way to sacrifice, a way to do without, even if the occasion doesn't call for it. The Martyr would choose a Spartan existence in a land of plenty, viewing discomfort as an ideal in and of itself.

By no means is this the total population of characters in Archetypeville. Typically, however, these characters represent an archetype that results from serious errors or distortions in our view of God.

Many perspectives act as a huge filter, rendering us blind and unable to recognize important things around us. Neurobiologists call this filter the Reticular Activating System (RAS). Here's how it works:

"The Reticular Activating System sits in your brain and acts as a customizable filter which adapts to different types of situations and reacts instantly.

The RAS can be seen as a bouncer at the door of your mind. Your beliefs tell the RAS what is or what is not important, chiefly making a list of all the information invited to the party, and your RAS then acts like the club bouncer letting whoever is on the list in and throwing the rest to the curb. Of the millions of bits of information that bombard our sensory system every second, our RAS will only let around 130 pieces of information per second in our conscious mind."

The obvious purpose of the RAS is to keep us from being overwhelmed from overstimulation.

The beliefs associated with our "perspective" at the moment, informs the RAS what to allow to enter our conscious awareness. At the same time, our perspective informs the RAS, which stimuli (facts, evidence, parts of reality) to which we will effectively remain blind.

At the time of an event, we may have embraced the values of a Victim, a Judge, a King or a Saboteur. Doing so blinds us to much of the reality around us, but upon later reflection, when we take a super slow motion approach, things change. In slow motion, we have the opportunity to reexamine a situation and put the evidence on trial. Viewed from multiple angles and subjected to corroborating evidence tests, the shaky evidence is exposed as unsound.

It may even appear ridiculous after serious examination.

The result is that our confidence in the underlying agreement disappears. The grip it has on us is loosened. We can now move from the shadow casting perspective of the Victim, King, etc., and have an unobstructed view of the facts surrounding the matter.

We may now see mounds of compelling and credible evidence for a loving God, none of which had ever before entered our conscious awareness.

Dismantling these agreements and confronting the pseudo-evidence with the superior evidence that we can now see is exactly the process described in 2 Corinthians chapter 10 verse 5.

"On the contrary, they have divine power to demolish strongholds. We demolish arguments and every pretension that sets itself up against the knowledge of God, and we take captive every thought to make it obedient to Christ."

Though this may sound like a violent episode, in truth the confronting is gentle, and the demolishing is just the result of agreements collapsing when the underlying evidence has been found lacking. We can now put our faith and confidence in the truths revealed by God, for the purpose of transforming our lives.

CHAPTER TWENTY-THREE
SETTING TRUTH AND BEAUTY FIRMLY
BEFORE YOU

"...set your hearts on things above, where Christ is, seated at the right hand of God. Set your minds on things above, not on earthly things."

Colossians 3:1-2

Have you ever noticed when you're riding a bicycle or driving a car that you tend to head in the direction in which you're looking? If you stare too long at something on the side of the road your bicycle or car will start to move in that direction.

We have similar responses whether we are looking at something or just holding the image of something in our mind's eye. Most of us think in images or pictures. When we consciously think of God, we want that image or picture to be true and beautiful, but most of our thoughts and actions are initiated on a subconscious level. Some social scientists say that as much as 90% of our thoughts, behaviors, and actions are initiated on an unconscious level. Dr. John A. Bargh, PhD. of Yale University, is a pioneer in the field of "automaticity" research, which studies the pervasive influence of the subconscious on human behavior. Leonard Mlodinow PhD. at Caltech University writes:

"Our subliminal brain is invisible to us, yet it influences our conscious experiences of the world in the most fundamental of ways: how we see ourselves and others, the meaning we attach to the everyday events of our lives, our ability to make the quick judgement calls and decisions that can sometimes mean the difference between life and death, and the actions we engage in as a result of all these instinctual experiences."

(How Your Unconscious Mind Rules Your Behavior, page 5)

That's why it's so important to have an accurate image of God, especially at the unconscious level. Here, in our heart of hearts, at the gut level, is where agreements are assembled, and strongholds are built.

If we pro-actively go about firmly setting the truth and beauty of God in our minds, it can radically change our whole view on life. Giving our attention to the truth and beauty of God creates such hopeful and empowering emotions. Our general demeanor improves. Life's events change from being demanding and threatening to grand opportunities. Life becomes a great treasure hunt.

We have spent a fair amount of time addressing our

erroneous views of God. We now have to turn our attention to the erroneous views we have of ourselves. When we see the folly of some disruptive agreement and no longer believe it represents who we truly are, where do we shift our attention? If I am not the Judge, nor the Victim, neither the Princess nor the King, then who exactly am I? From what perspective would God have me view Him, life and everything else?

This is what the Psalms say regarding humans in general:

"...what is man that you are mindful of them,

the son of man that you care for them?

You have made them a little lower than the angels

and crowned them with glory and honor.

You made them rulers over the works of your hands;

you put everything under their feet:

all flocks and herds, and the animals of the wild,

the birds in the sky, and the fish in the sea,

all that swim the paths of the seas."

Psalm 8:4

How can we ever suffer from poor self-esteem with a resume like that?

But wait, there's more! For those who believe God's message and are Christ followers, the description of our true identity is even more lofty.

The list of passages that communicate our elevated identity in Christ is too long to include here. A study on the subject would reveal much to encourage the heart. Below are five passages representative of dozens of others that communicate the same message.

"Therefore, if anyone is in Christ, he is a new creation. The old has passed away; behold, the new has come."

2 Corinthians 5:17

"I have been crucified with Christ. It is no longer I who live, but Christ who lives in me. And the life I now live in the flesh I live by faith in the Son of God, who loved me and gave himself for me."

Galatians 2:20

"But you are a chosen race, a royal priesthood, a holy nation, a people for his own possession, that you may proclaim the excellencies of him who called you out of darkness into his marvelous light."

1 Peter 2:9

"No longer do I call you servants, for the servant does not know what his master is doing; but I have called you friends, for all that I have heard from my Father I have made known to you."

John 15:15

"There is therefore now no condemnation for those who are in Christ Jesus."

Romans 8:1

Can you even find the courage to own fully who God says you are in Christ?

If you find it difficult, it might be because the opposite view has permeated church culture for centuries. I don't know how it began or why it persists to this day, but the tradition goes something like this:

As believers in Jesus, we are all just sinners saved by grace. The essence of who we are at the core is weak, no good, prone to sin, and not to be trusted.

I don't know about you, but that does not sound like a child of God, co-heir with Christ or "more than a conqueror." This much we can know: if God describes us in such glowing terms, then this less than, inadequate, low-life identity is contrived and merely a mental construct. We made it up ourselves.

In Jeremiah 17:5-8, this is what the Lord says:

"Cursed is the one who trusts in man,
who draws strength from mere flesh
and whose heart turns away from the Lord.

That person will be like a bush in the wastelands;
they will not see prosperity when it comes.

They will dwell in the parched places of the desert,
in a salt land where no one lives.

But blessed is the one who trusts in the Lord,
whose confidence is in him.

They will be like a tree planted by the water
that sends out its roots by the stream.

It does not fear when heat comes;
its leaves are always green.

It has no worries in a year of drought
and never fails to bear fruit."

We are not to put faith in our own construct of ourselves,
but in what the Lord declares he has made of us.

As you work through this, remember to stay in peace, joy,
and gratitude. Neither self-condemnation nor the blaming
of others will be our strength or bring about the righteous
life God desires.

Constantly see yourself acting, speaking, thinking, and feeling like the kind of person God declares you are in Him.

"Let love and faithfulness never leave you;
bind them around your neck,
write them on the tablet of your heart.

Then you will win favor and a good name
in the sight of God and man."

Proverbs 3:3-4

"A good man brings good things out of the good stored up in him, and an evil man brings evil things out of the evil stored up in him."

(If "stored up good" had a physical location in your body, where would it be located and what would it look like?)

Matthew 12:35

"Above all else, guard your heart, for everything you do flows from it."

Proverbs 4:23

"Whoever sows to please their flesh, from the flesh will reap destruction; whoever sows to please the Spirit, from the Spirit will reap eternal life."

Galatians 6:8

"For as he thinketh in his heart, so is he."

Proverbs 23:7

Agreement dismantled, perspective shifted, now what? I bet you wouldn't be surprised to learn that this process is not a one-time thing. As you're going about your business, and an old agreement from the past rears its ugly head, you just wave at it, acknowledge that it's there, and give it no energy or attention. Just let it die a slow but steady death from neglect.

In 2 Corinthians 5:7, we are encouraged to, "Walk by faith and not by sight." Of course, there are many aspects to walking by faith. One that we will fix our attention on here is a requirement to walking by faith. That requirement is the ability to fix a thought, image, or principal in our mind's eye and move in that direction, ignoring the stimuli flooding our physical senses. This concept is captured in the adage, "to march to the beat of a different drum," or, "You gotta bring your own weather."

I had a situation on my way to work that illustrates the need to ignore certain things to walk by faith. Most days I take the commuter train from downtown Los Angeles Union Station to Chatsworth on the outskirts of the county. When I first started commuting this way, I had difficulty with the vending machine that sold the tickets. With most vending machine-like devices, when you press a key, a sound is emitted that lets you know the input was received. When it was time to enter my four-digit password into the ticketing machine, it appeared that it was not working. I pressed the digit and waited. Nothing. I pressed another digit, then another and waited more. Then I heard the tone for the first digit that I pressed. I realized that I would have to enter all four digits with no immediate feedback as to whether or not the machine was receiving information.

A lightbulb went off in my brain. Faithful living is a lot like this. You can decide what you're going to do, and then go about doing it faithfully. There may be no immediate feedback indicating what you're doing is going to be effective. When it comes to the ticket machine at Union Station, I had to set my mind. I told myself to just enter those four digits in a row no matter what the machine did, or sounded like. I decided I would take the same approach to life. There are things I need to do, ways I need to be, responses I need to have, and things I need to initiate, that I will have to do while either getting no or strange and confusing feedback.

We need to anticipate encounters we are likely to have based on our average schedule and routine. Given the possibility of these events, we need to set in our minds ahead of time what they mean to us and how we're going to conduct ourselves. We will have a faithful image of the following in our minds before we experience them:

- How are we going to be around family?

- How are we going to be at work?

- How are we going to respond to strangers?

- How are we going to respond to those asking for a favor?

On an average day, I interact with people of all sorts. Some are a refreshing delight; others, not so much. To expand my joy in the company of the not-so-refreshing, I remind myself of the truth regarding the person I'm encountering:

1. We are one humanity.

2. Their business is not my business.

3. They don't owe me kindness, consideration, or respect.

4. Prayer is aided by peace and joy.

5. Be thankful, always.

6. Drama can be funny.

7. It's their story.

8. They don't know what they are doing.

9. You catch more flies with honey.

10. If you only knew what they are overcoming.

11. There are so many better things to consider.

12. Fix your eyes on Jesus.

13. Count your blessings.

14. They are made in the image of God.

15. Share your faith.

16. Mean people are usually in pain.

17. Loud people are often the loneliest.

18. Criticism corrodes from within.

19. They're family.

20. Be curious about their take on things.

"So we fix our eyes not on what is seen, but on what is unseen, since what is seen is temporary, but what is unseen is eternal."

2 Corinthians 4:18

The agreements, mental constructs, and false personas of our minds are only temporary. They will pass away with time and neglect, but the truths on which we will set our minds are eternal.

The apostle Paul exhorts,

"Finally, brothers, whatever is true, whatever is noble, whatever is right, whatever is pure, whatever is lovely, whatever is admirable--if anything is excellent or praiseworthy--think about such things. Whatever you have learned or received or heard from me, or seen in me-- put it into practice. And the God of peace will be with you."

Philippians 4:8-9

These final exhortations concern all aspects of life, the internal and the external, what we think and what we do. Let's give our attention to one of the things that Paul lists: "Finally, brothers, whatever is true, ...think about such things" (Philippians 4:8).

So what is true?

Romans 1:20 says:

"For since the creation of the world God's invisible qualities—his eternal power and divine nature—have been clearly seen, being understood from what has been made, so that men are without excuse."

I hope it is well-established in your mind and faith that everything in the Bible is true. It reveals volumes about God. The Bible proclaims that many things outside of its pages also reveal God. Psalm 19 proclaims:

"The heavens declare the glory of God;
the skies proclaim the work of his hands.

Day after day they pour forth speech;
night after night they display knowledge.

There is no speech or language
where their voice is not heard.

Their voice goes out into all the earth, their words to the
ends of the world."

Psalm 19:1-4

Jesus taught that the truth would set you free. The Apostle
John describes Jesus in contrast to Moses. He said, "For
the law was given through Moses; grace and truth came
through Jesus Christ" (John 1:17). Grace and truth are not
in opposition to each other. Jesus brought the grace of
God, which is the truth. He did not bring the grace of God
and the truth about how we fall short. The law that comes
through Moses did a stellar job of that. The problem with
the law is that it was not suited to redeem or renew the
law breaker. Jesus is not playing the good cop bad cop
role. Like the parallelism used with many of the proverbs,
where one statement merely expands upon the other, John
ascribes to Jesus grace and truth.

Consider the many passages below, where Jesus expressly
states that he is going to tell his audience "the truth." You'll
notice that the truth is about God's love, the believer's
reward, the effect of our faith, etc. When Jesus set out to

tell the people the truth, it had little or nothing to do with persuading them of their sinfulness.

Matthew 10:42

"And if anyone gives even a cup of cold water to one of these little ones because he is my disciple, I tell you the truth; he will certainly not lose his reward."

Matthew 17:20

"He replied, 'Because you have so little faith. I tell you the truth, if you have faith as small as a mustard seed, you can say to this mountain, 'Move from here to there' and it will move. Nothing will be impossible for you.' But this kind does not go out except by prayer and fasting."

Matthew 18:18

"I tell you the truth, whatever you bind on earth will be bound in heaven, and whatever you loose on earth will be loosed in heaven."

Matthew 21:21

Jesus replied, "I tell you the truth, if you have faith and do not doubt, not only can you do what was done to the fig tree, but also you can say to this mountain, 'Go, throw yourself into the sea,' and it will be done.

"Who then is the faithful and wise servant, whom the

master has put in charge of the servants in his household to give them their food at the proper time? It will be good for that servant whose master finds him doing so when he returns. I tell you the truth, he will put him in charge of all his possessions.

Matthew 25:45

"The King will reply, 'Truly I tell you, whatever you did for one of the least of these brothers and sisters of mine, you did for me.'"

Matthew 25:40

"He will reply, 'I tell you the truth, whatever you did not do for one of the least of these, you did not do for me.'

"I tell you the truth," Jesus replied, "no one who has left home or brothers or sisters or mother or father or children or fields for me and the gospel will fail to receive a hundred times as much in this present age (homes, brothers, sisters, mothers, children and fields—and with them, persecutions) and in the age to come, eternal life. But many who are first will be last, and the last first."

Luke 23:43

"Jesus answered him, 'I tell you the truth, today you will be with me in paradise.'"

John 1:51

"He then added, 'I tell you the truth, you shall see heaven open, and the angels of God ascending and descending on the Son of Man.'"

John 5:19

"Jesus gave them this answer: 'I tell you the truth, the Son can do nothing by himself; he can do only what he sees his Father doing, because whatever the Father does the Son also does.'"

John 5:24

"I tell you the truth, whoever hears my word and believes him who sent me has eternal life and will not be condemned; he has crossed over from death to life."

John 5:25

"I tell you the truth, a time is coming and has now come when the dead will hear the voice of the Son of God and those who hear will live."

John 6:47

"I tell you the truth, he who believes has everlasting life."

John 6:53

Jesus said to them, "I tell you the truth, unless you eat the flesh of the Son of Man and drink his blood, you have no life in you.

To the Jews who had believed him, Jesus said, "If you hold to my teaching, you are really my disciples. Then you will know the truth, and the truth will set you free."

John 8:51

"I tell you the truth, if anyone keeps my word, he will never see death."

John 12:24

"I tell you the truth, unless a kernel of wheat falls to the ground and dies, it remains only a single seed. But if it dies, it produces many seeds."

John 14:6

"Jesus answered, 'I am the way and the truth and the life. No one comes to the Father except through me.'"

John 14:12

"I tell you the truth, anyone who has faith in me will do what I have been doing. He will do even greater things than these, because I am going to the Father."

John 16:13

"But when he, the Spirit of truth, comes, he will guide you into all truth. He will not speak on his own; he will speak only what he hears, and he will tell you what is yet to come."

John 16:23

"In that day you will no longer ask me anything. I tell you the truth; my Father will give you whatever you ask in my name."

We should run to the truth like two lovers running toward each other with their arms wide open on a beach.

This is the truth we are to embrace. Set the truth of the father's love before you. Set the truth of your identity as a cherished child deep in your heart.

Have a clear image of your desired quietness and trust along with an eager expectation of good from God. Do not give any attention or energy to what you don't want.

I invite you to pray and ask God to use these truths from Jesus to transform and equip our souls for faithfulness today.

What is true about all that took place yesterday and last week?

1. God is working all things out for the good of those who love Him.

2. Any and all good that you did for people has resulted in a reward kept secure in heaven for you.

3. God is using all the trials, struggles, troubles, pains and difficulties of yesterday to create a stronger more faithful you.

4. The sins committed are forgiven and separated from you as far as the east is from the west. They are not remembered by God. They are not from your heart, but rather are the death throes of a sinful flesh that has been crucified. The fruits of yesterday and last week are for your good, a greater reward, added strength, mercy and grace. I'll take that any day of the week!

Now that yesterday is secured away, what about today?

What is the truth about this moment in time?

Now is all you have or have ever had. You can do absolutely nothing in the past, however recent. And you can do nothing in the future, however near. You only have right now. You can only eat, sleep, work, serve, love or believe right now. As reference earlier;

"Our task is not to know what lies dimly in the future, but to do what lies clearly at hand."

It's the present moment, "what lies clearly at hand," over which we have any influence.

What else is playing in the background of your mind? What is the theme music of your mind? What image is on the desktop of your mind? What is the backdrop against which all the thoughts emerge? This background picture reflects what we hold to be true regarding God's activity or inactivity for our benefit in the world around us.

Jesus says, "My Father is always working." Since God is always working, what spiritual activity is surrounding you right now? Within a two block radius of where you are at present, what is going on? We assume birds are flying even if we can't see them. We expect cars to be traveling down streets and people to be walking around, though we may not be able to see or hear them. We just know that something is going on out there. The question is how do we come to a place where we always picture and assume the activities of heaven are "going on out there" on the desktops of our minds?

The Bible records that Jacob went to sleep one night in what he thought was an ordinary field. After an amazing dream, he woke up realizing that this field was the very "gate of heaven." The angels were entering and departing our world from that very spot he had slept. Are you also at the "gate of heaven"? Are there angels entering and departing our world from your very spot? As with Elijah, are there chariots of fire surrounding you?

Try this. Read Job 38:4-40:2 out loud to yourself 3-4 times a day for a week. Express to God throughout the day the things you observe that you know are Him at work. Sing a song in your morning devotional time with God that tells of his working in the moments of your day. Send a friend a note, letter, email or text about how you have seen God at work today and how it builds your faith.

God loves you.

God is near.

God is leading you.

God is in you, creating the righteous will and desires of your heart.

You are surrounded by God on every side.

"In him, we live and move and have our being."

Acts 17:28

God alone knows what the future holds, so why make up a negative story in your mind?

Jesus is interceding in prayer for you.

Angels are charged with your aid and protection.

SECTION FOUR: OVERCOMING THE OBSTACLES TO FOLLOWING THE SPIRIT

CHAPTER TWENTY-FOUR
THE PRACTICE OF HEARING AND HEEDING

"The function of prayer is not to influence God, but rather to change the nature of the one who prays."

— Soren Kierkegaard

"God speaks in the silence of the heart. Listening is the beginning of prayer."

Mother Teresa

Now, we have heard the unmistakable voice of God and then the obstacles magically appear. These are the challenges which must be overcome once we've clearly heard and discerned God speaking to us.

One of the first and most common obstacles we will encounter is simply fear. This is a fear that some harm is going to come to us as we endeavor to do what God has called us to. This is the kind of obstacle that Ananias had to overcome when the voice of God clearly spoke to him and told him to reach out to the first church's version of a serial killer, Saul of Tarsus, and share his faith because he was going to be an instrument in the hand of God.

The next common obstacle to address is inconvenience. We are on our way to perform some task when we discern that unmistakable small voice calling us to do something God intends for us. This is the obstacle that's addressed in the parable of the wedding banquet. God sent out his invitation to the surrounding people to attend his son's wedding. The responses ranged from, "I have just bought a field, and I must go see it", to, "I just got married, so I can't come." Business is not just a modern phenomenon. Those who would walk with God have always had to deal with divine interruptions. The key to navigating these situations is to remember that God has plans to prosper us and not to harm us. Any inconvenience or loss we suffer by attending to His call will always pale in comparison to the joy and satisfaction of being used by Him.

Next on our list of obstacles to address is common but isn't often thought about: resentment. There are times when God will call us to reach out to someone we don't like, to serve someone we don't think is deserving or to extend an invitation to hear the gospel to someone we believe is working actively against God. This is the obstacle that Jonah encountered when he heard the voice of God speaking to him to go preach to the Ninevites. The Ninevites were not exactly on friendly terms with Israel and had a reputation of being an aggressive, ungodly, violent, immoral people who had heard God's will before and rejected it many times. Jonah knew many of his countrymen had suffered at the hands of the Ninevites. Look at Jonah chapter 5 and we can see him sulking under a tree which offered little shade. He was resentful that God had called him to extend a hand of fellowship to a people like the Ninevites.

This next hurdle doesn't apply to everyone, but many of us can intimately relate to it. That is the obstacle concerning what other people think. We've heard God's voice and it's within our capacity to act. This task however can't be completed in private. Other people will be watching. What are they going to say? You work with some of these people. Noah faced this challenge. Think about it. Literally everybody in his world had an opinion about his building this ark. How did he resist such potential pressure? What made him feel like he was right and everybody who criticized his actions were off base? Noah had a firm grasp on who God was. It may very well be that the Bible doesn't express a lot of angst on the his part because there wasn't any.

One of the most well-known Bible characters who struggled with the cost of following the voice of God was the Rich Young Ruler. He had studied the scriptures and had a great command of them. He set out for an audience with Jesus. When he found him, Jesus told him to go sell all he had and give to the poor. Only then would he have treasures in Heaven. Then he was told to follow Jesus. The Bible says his face fell and he went away sad because he was a person of great wealth. The problem for the rich, young man is he had a low estimation of the wealth and riches in store for him as one of Jesus' followers. How many of us go away sad if a salesman at a Tesla dealership told us he could let one go for $5. There would be no sadness because we estimate the value of the Tesla to be far greater than whatever amount of money we had in our pocket.

The Old Testament character Naaman struggled momentarily with following God because the instructions he received didn't make sense to him. Eventually he gained the victory. Naaman had been struck with a form of leprosy that had left him disfigured and unsightly. He was told by the prophet of God (speaking as the voice of God) to dip himself seven times in the Jordan River. Now, the Jordan River wasn't exactly the Crystal Springs. Nevertheless, it wasn't going to be the physical and chemical attributes of the water that we're going to accomplish a miracle. It would have been the power of God activated through the faith of Naaman. Eventually he was persuaded, and he lowered himself into the Jordan River where he dipped seven times. On the seventh time, the Bible reports that he came up from the water and his skin was like that of a newborn. I wonder how many miracles I've missed out on over the course of my life simply because some direction didn't make sense to me.

Fortunately for us, we have been strengthened with the truth and equipped with the tools and skills needed to identify, neutralize, and overcome the potential impediment to the kind of relationship with God long before we were born.

CONCLUSION

God's desire for a close and personal relationship with each of us endures to this very hour. He longs for and is willing to take up residence in our hearts to comfort and lead us from within.

We cooperate with God's desire largely to the degree that we view Him as safe, loving, and with the intention to bring us good. Many of us have misinterpreted the cause of painful and disturbing events in our lives and allowed them to cast a shadow on our thoughts regarding God. We understand the obstructive and destructive nature of those distorted images of God.

From a place of acceptance and peace, we now have a way to identify and correct those erroneous views. The evidence for our conclusions about God is tested for their validity in the light of the overwhelming evidence for God's love. As a result, we see God as the marvelous and loving being that he is. We also come to see the truth of our own elevated and empowered identity in Him.

We are not the Victim. We are not the Judge. We are not a sin. For those in Christ, we are the cherished and beloved children of God. As such, we wait patiently and listen attentively for that "still small voice." We embrace the sentiment of young Samuel and say, "Speak Lord, for your servant is listening." And when we hear God saying to us, "This is the way, walk in it," we respond faithfully as young Mary said to the angel Gabriel, "May it be to me as you have spoken."

Welcome to the community of Spirit-led hearts.

Let the adventure begin!

Made in the USA
Coppell, TX
31 August 2022